Why do I pray?

My heart
has heard God say,
"Come and talk with me."
And my heart responds,
"Lord, I am coming."
Psalm 27:8

Prayer

&

Me

By Susan McGeown

Published By

Faith Inspired Books

www.susanmcgeown.com

Faith Inspired Books

Published by Faith Inspired Books

www.susanmcgeown.com

ISBN-10: 0983536090

ISBN-13: 978-0-9835360-9-3

Scripture verses quoted are from the author's personal favorite translation, the New Living Translation published by Tyndale House Publishers, Inc. 2008 Study Edition.

For additions, deletions, corrections, or clarifications please contact Susan McGeown at the above address.

Bibliographic and footnote credit appears at the end of this work.

Table of Contents

Prayer

It comes in all shapes and sizes.

There's the prayer that you pray just before you walk into the big meeting to quell your nervousness, there's the prayer you say beside the bedside of a sick loved one, there's the prayer you murmur when you're walking to your car in the dark and you're frightened, and there's the prayer you utter watching the terrible events on the evening news. Then there are prayers you say at meals, during church worship, and by rote that you have learned from childhood. And there are formal prayers in which you set aside a time and commune personally with your God.

> God, show me what you are doing today, and how I can be part of it.
>
> *(Yancey, 168)*

Perhaps you do some of these and maybe you do all of these. Prayer is the opportunity for the created to commune with the creator. A formal definition of 'prayer' is "a reverent petition made to God" and was recorded in the Middle English as 'preide' (to ask earnestly) as early as 1290 A.D. and the Old French as 'preier' (to request) as early as 880 A.D. Synonyms such as supplication, worship, benediction, blessing, petition, request, invocation, appeal … all give us further glimpses into the wide reaching arena that the word 'prayer' addresses.

The range of prayer is a little like clothing. There is the comfortable stuff that we wear whenever we can, the acceptable public clothing that we wear to go out in public, and there is the formal and professional attire we wear when we are attempting to look our very best. All are important in defining who and what we are.

This book seeks to help you understand prayer in the manner in which God intended prayer to be: as a vital, privileged, powerful weapon. Look at it as an opportunity for you to establish a personal relationship with the creator of the universe and in doing so achieve a purposeful direction for your life that will lead to incredible joy and ultimate gratification.

I fall to my knees and pray to the Father, the Creator of everything in heaven and on earth.

I pray that from his glorious, unlimited resources he will empower you with inner strength through his Spirit.

Then Christ will make his home in your hearts as you trust in him. Your roots will grow down into God's love and keep you strong.

And may you have the power to understand, as all God's people should, how wide, how long, how high, and how deep his love is.

May you experience the love of Christ, though it is too great to understand fully.

Then you will be made complete with all the fullness of life and power that comes from God.

Now all glory to God, who is able, through his mighty power at work within us, to accomplish infinitely more than we might ask or think.

Ephesians 3:14-20

Prayer & My Questions

THINK: If your questions about prayer are not addressed in this book, where can you go to find the answers?

I asked for people to submit questions to guide me in the direction to which I was going to go for this study. Below are the excellent questions I received and what I had in mind as I put together this book.

Yet, what questions do _you_ have about prayer? In my experience as a teacher for over thirty years, questions are the very heart of discovery. Asking questions _and then seeking answers_ is the key to intellectual and spiritual growth. If the questions listed below do not address what you wish to understand about prayer than make a commitment to yourself to further explore this topic. At the end of this book are a few resources that are highly recommended.

Prayer In General

1. What does it do? What's in it for me, both now and eventually?
2. What does it do for those I pray for?
3. Is it really just an empty activity of words and thoughts to someone, something that I can't touch or see?

Prayer and Doing It The Right Way

4. What can/should spur me to pray? Or should I plan a time to do it?

5. Types of prayer...Group, individual, family, friends, grace before meals, prayer to start a meeting. Why, how do they work for a participant(s)? Methods...Silent, vocal, written word, sung, responsorial, spur of the moment, planned and/or repetitive....Places...Church, car, home, restaurant, on the street, in a doc's office, bedside. What types/methods/places result in the most positive feeling at the moment/long term? Is that the point? Or should something else be the "result?"

6. I want to know how to pray the CORRECT way. I want to claim the promises of God according to the Bible. I want His will revealed to me. I want the same kind of power that is described in the New Testament available to me so that I can face all challenges that life throws at me.

7. Am I praying correctly? ("Be careful what you pray for, because you may just get it.")

8. We're supposed to pray constantly. If I don't pray for a day, will He stop answering my prayers?

9. Conversation in prayer by stating what we are going through and asking for guidance as well as expressing gratitude and continued blessings seems about right. Are we supposed to pray about the same things every day?

10. Sometimes "blessed" or "fortunate" people don't really have empathy for others going through troubling times. Maybe they feel they're blessed due to something they're doing "right" that others aren't doing. They won't know 'til things happen to them; although I would never, never wish anything bad on anyone. On the other hand, some people appear so faith-based that bad things don't seem

to phase them; they concentrate on their many blessings instead. The Bible says something about not worrying. So how do we not sound desperate and redundant, and do prayers really matter?

11. I say a very long prayer every night, basically the same one. Does God want me to shorten it on those nights I am very tired and just going through the words? Is less, more?

12. Will the Lord's Prayer plus the names of folks who need healing and the regions that need peace suffice? Or does God want details? I do talk to Him all day but the formal prayer is at night.

Prayer, God's Will & Me

13. How do I accept results that were not what I had hoped/prayed for? More prayer?

14. I want to learn about effective prayer. I don't mean how to get what I want, more like how to be what HE wants!

15. Praying for "God's Will" seems so simple and generic. Also scary. What if God's will isn't what we had in mind?

16. I'm sometimes tired, frustrated and feel I don't know how to pray anymore. How do we pray "right" and accept outcomes that are hurtful?

17. Is there supposed to be a silver lining from life's hurt down the road or we're supposed to learn a lesson?

18. I had someone say to me once that no praying will help, because God has it all planned out ahead of time. Are prayers ever really answered, or is everything that happens God's will?

Prayer and When Tragedy Strikes

19. I don't believe there are certain "good" people on which tragedy doesn't befall. We are all subject to it, some more than others due to chosen actions, but sometimes it seems like "how could God have let this happen?"

20. People that have been fortunate thus far are grateful and feel blessed. But what happens when things fall apart? Do they suddenly begin searching for answers as to what could possibly have caused this to happen to a prayerful, good person?

My Questions

List below the questions _you_ have about prayer.

THINK: Have you asked God to help you have a deeper understanding of Him and what He needs from you?

---

1. Prayer & God

Before we begin this study we must lay a foundation about what we believe about God. That attempt, in and of itself, is a complete study! However, in very basic language I've outlined five facts are the key building blocks regarding how we should approach prayer.

> **THINK:** What is my perception of God? What are God's key attributes? What does God want from me? What is the evidence of God in my life?

Elijah's Prayer of Despair

God's prophet Elijah had witnessed God's phenomenal power and glory. God had spoken with him directly, guiding him successfully against numerous confrontations against the evil Queen Jezebel and her equally despicable husband, King Ahab. But when the malicious acts Elijah witnessed overwhelmed him and his life was threatened, Elijah ran away. Even as he ran, God cared for him. Finally, the two had a conversation. After all he had witnessed, Elijah needed to be reminded of exactly Who the Lord God of Israel was. (I Kings 19:10-18, NLT)

> *But the LORD said to him, "What are you doing here, Elijah?"*

[10] *Elijah replied, "I have zealously served the* LORD *God Almighty. But the people of Israel have broken their covenant with you, torn down your altars, and killed every one of your prophets. I am the only one left, and now they are trying to kill me, too."*

[11] *"Go out and stand before me on the mountain,"* *the* LORD *told him. And as Elijah stood there, the* LORD *passed by, and a mighty windstorm hit the mountain. It was such a terrible blast that the rocks were torn loose, but the* LORD *was not in the wind. After the wind there was an earthquake, but the* LORD *was not in the earthquake.* [12] *And after the earthquake there was a fire, but the* LORD *was not in the fire. And after the fire there was the sound of a gentle whisper.* [13] *When Elijah heard it, he wrapped his face in his cloak and went out and stood at the entrance of the cave.*

And a voice said, "What are you doing here, Elijah?"

[14] *He replied again, "I have zealously served the* LORD *God Almighty. But the people of Israel have broken their covenant with you, torn down your altars, and killed every one of your prophets. I am the only one left, and now they are trying to kill me, too."*

[15] *Then the* LORD *told him, "Go back the same way you came, and travel to the wilderness of Damascus. When you arrive there, anoint Hazael to*

be king of Aram. [16] Then anoint Jehu grandson of Nimshi to be king of Israel, and anoint Elisha son of Shaphat from the town of Abel-meholah to replace you as my prophet. [17] Anyone who escapes from Hazael will be killed by Jehu, and those who escape Jehu will be killed by Elisha! [18] Yet I will preserve 7,000 others in Israel who have never bowed down to Baal or kissed him!"

God Facts

Fact #1. God's ways are perfect. God cannot make mistakes. God is all knowing, all powerful, and has no beginning and no end.

Based on this:

    a. The ultimate authority in my life must be God's eternity.

    b. I must operate by God's timeline.

    a. The laws of genetics should only be disbanded according to God's timeline.

    b. I should want God to fulfill only the prayers that He thinks are best.

Fact #2: God desires a personal relationship with each one of us. Because God is not hindered by time, God can be with each one of us at all times. The best way for me to communicate with God is through prayer.

Based on this:

    a. My purpose for praying should be to establish a close personal relationship with God.

b. My prayers should help me keep on the right track spiritually, make me feel closer to God, help me better understand myself, and help me understand God's will better.

c. My prayers should resemble a personal conversation with a close, dear, loving friend.

d. I should expect every single one of my prayers to be answered.

Fact #3: Our prayers are the only way to communicate with God.

Based on this:

> A God unbound by our rules of time has the ability to invest in every person on earth.
>
> *(Yancey, 49)*

a. My prayers should be honest, personal, and uniquely me.

b. I should not compare myself to others.

c. God welcomes all honest emotion.

d. I should focus on candid subject matter, authentic expression, and my distinctive style.

e. I must take responsibility for the quality of my prayer life.

f. I need to understand what I should and shouldn't pray for.

g. I should expect my prayers to make a difference.

Fact #4: God wants to hear our prayers.

Remember these biblical truths when you doubt the need and power of prayer:

a. Jesus prayed continually throughout his time on earth and regularly sought time in prayer for strength, direction, and comfort.

b. Prayer was regularly the primary communication through which God has communicated wants, needs, and requirements.

c. Prayer enables us to see the world from a godly rather than human perspective.

d. Our free will enables us to accept or reject God. In entering into prayer with God we initiate a relationship.

Fact #5: Prayers should never be meant to change God's Mind.

Prayer is meant to change *our* mind,

a. To understand God's Will.

b. To help us align ourselves with God's Plans.

c. To help us discover God's Purpose for our lives.

d. To help us view others and the world from God's Perspective rather than our own.

THINK: Where is there time in your day to spend some quality time with God? How can you establish a routine where you meet daily to talk with God?

Why do I pray?

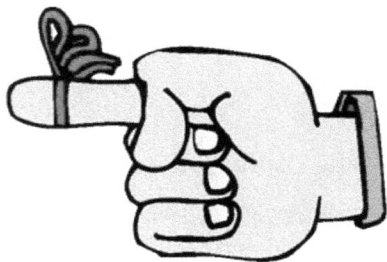

I pray not to tell God what He needs to know or remind him of things that He has forgotten. I pray because prayer gives me the opportunity to *finally* care about things from the same perspective as God. **Prayer allows me to see others as God sees them.**

2. Prayer, Posture, & Style

The first thing I need to tell you regarding this aspect of prayer is to R-E-L-A-X. Our prayers should be as personal and unique as we are as individuals. The worst thing you can do regarding your prayer life is compare yourself to others and attempt to be something you are not. Being your honest self is the best way to start when you approach God in prayer.

> **THINK:** What appeals to you the most: starting your day off with prayer or ending your day in prayer?

Mary's Prayer of Praise

She was poor. She was young. She was unmarried. She was pregnant even though she was a virgin. Mary found herself in a situation no one on the planet has ever been in before or since. And yet, her response was prayer – effortlessly, immediately, willingly. That's the only true posture and style we need to concern ourselves with really. (Luke 1:46-55)

> [6] *Mary responded,*
>
> *"Oh, how my soul praises the Lord.*
> [47] *How my spirit rejoices in God my Savior!*

*⁴⁸ For he took notice of his lowly servant girl, and
from now on all generations will call me blessed.
⁴⁹ For the Mighty One is holy, and he has done great
things for me.
⁵⁰ He shows mercy from generation to generation
to all who fear him.
⁵¹ His mighty arm has done tremendous things! He
has scattered the proud and haughty ones.
⁵² He has brought down princes from their thrones
and exalted the humble.
⁵³ He has filled the hungry with good things and
sent the rich away with empty hands.
⁵⁴ He has helped his servant Israel and remembered
to be merciful.
⁵⁵ For he made this promise to our ancestors, to
Abraham and his children forever."*

Silent vs. Aloud

<u>Praying silently is to praying aloud as private chats are to public speeches.</u>
There is a distinct difference between prayers said aloud for all to hear and personal prayers said quietly, privately (and probably silently) between you and God. You should never, ever compare your personal prayers to anything you hear prayed aloud. It's like comparing apples to oranges; they may be both fruit but they have a whole different taste.

Praying silently to God is a close, intimate conversation. Praying aloud, while it addresses God, also includes the present praying community. Each have their own vital role and perform an important spiritual service.

Praying aloud was distinctly more difficult for me than praying silently and for years it was a painful, heart palpating process when I was faced with it. Practice does help. I was never, ever able to master the fancy prayers you hear ministers do all the time. What I did master *was the ability to be comfortable with my own style.* If praying aloud is absolutely not for you then put it aside for now; wrap it up in a nice little bow and store it carefully on a shelf for the time being.

A majority of this study will be regarding silent, personal prayer.

Posture

He'll take you any way He can get you.

Whether you're on your knees or standing in line at the grocery store, God welcomes your prayers. Never doubt that. Yet if prayer is the most important time for you to get to really know God, finding a time, place, and posture where you're comfortable, focused, and uninterrupted would certainly mean that the quality of our prayers must be based on when and where we are. While God welcomes your earnest prayer said quickly as you dash into your important corporate meeting, God also wants some undivided, quality one on one time

> The habit of not praying is far more difficult to break than the habit of praying.
>
> *(Yancey, 202)*

with you, too. You need to carve out a time in your busy life where not only can you talk at length with God but that you can sit quietly and listen to what He has to tell you, too. You need to make sure that you are having a dialogue with God; not a monologue. However you manage that can be as creative as necessary.

A prayer life always spoken on the fly, always in the midst of disaster, and always a litany of one-sided requests from you is nowhere near as close and as vital as it should be. Think about your friendships. What friend do you rely on, trust, and love the most? Is it the one who only calls you when she needs an emergency babysitter or when she's got just two minutes to send you a brief text or email? Or is it the friend who knows by the sound of your voice that you're upset, who you've shared endless laughter and tears with, and who you require hours to catch up with when you finally get time to talk? *Your prayer life with God should be like a close, personal friendship.*

Style

<u>Consistency is far more important than style.</u>

- Prayer journaling.
- Prayer at bedtime.
- Prayer in the car on the way to work.
- Voicing the Lord's Prayer aloud each morning as you walk the dog.
- Sitting silently in your favorite chair with a cup of tea each afternoon.
- Prayer first thing in the morning before you roll out of bed.
- Reading scripture.

Finding a time and a place and a way to communicate with God on a faithful basis is The Most Important Thing when it comes to establishing a vital prayer life. It will probably be as unique as you are and it's never wise to compare yourself to others. I *do* like asking people how they pray; it opens up ideas that I didn't even think to consider.

In addition, did you know that there are all *kinds* of prayer? (You'll might be surprised at how many you have already done.) Here's a brief list; there are certainly others but I have chosen just the most common. (I talk a bit more and provide scriptural support for each of these styles in the section entitled "Types of Prayers"):

- **Supplication Prayers** involve making a conscious decision to pray about something instead of worry about something. You give all your fear, anxiety, and impatience to God.

- **Believing Prayers** constantly look for God to do the impossible, extraordinary, and unbelievable in your life.

- **Revealing Prayers** involve asking God to help you understand something. Rather than trying to convince God of something; you ask God to clarify things for you.

- **Interceding Prayers** are specific requests for those in need. You pray fervently for someone but trust God for the results.

- **Corporate Prayers** are prayers done with others.

- **Persevering Prayers** are prayers that you say continually and involve patience, faith, and waiting.

- **Thanksgiving/Worship Prayers** are prayers that express thanks for all that God has done.

- **Consecration Prayers** are prayers where you are set apart from others and determine to follow God's will.

How many of these types of prayers have you done over the course of your life?

Always remember this important fact with regard to prayer: *How* you do it: aloud, silent, sitting, kneeling, or riding on the train isn't nearly as important as *the way* you do it: with an earnest desire to share as well as to listen.

THINK: Where and when do you pray most regularly? What kind of prayer do you do voice frequently? The next time you pray, try a different style, a different place, and a different time. You might be surprised what you discover!

Why do I pray?

I pray because I believe it is the very best way to get to know God better. I find it astonishing that **the God of the Universe desires a relationship with me ... how cool is that?**

3. Prayer & The Proper Attitude

THINK: Is it possible to get prayer wrong? Is it possible to do things that make your prayers more powerful and effective?

Jude' Prayer of Praise

In the New Testament, Jude's letter is at the very end, right before the book of Revelation and he is entirely focused on the danger of false teachers and the damage they can do. It's a short letter and he finishes with a beautiful benediction, praising God. This attitude of utter love, reverence, and confidence is the best attitude we can bring with us when we pray. (Jude 1:24-25)

> *24 Now all glory to God, who is able to keep you from falling away and will bring you with great joy into his glorious presence without a single fault.*
> *25 All glory to him who alone is God, our Savior through Jesus Christ our Lord. All glory, majesty, power, and authority are his before all time, and in the present, and beyond all time! Amen.*

Is there a right way and a wrong way to pray?

It all depends on the attitude.

The quick answer to that question is yes and no. God doesn't really care about your articulating prowess. He doesn't need you to sound a certain way or use a certain set of words. But God absolutely cares about what attitude you have when you enter into prayer. It's not as easy as you think, but it's also not that difficult. *Prayer requires thought.*

- **FORGIVENESS:** We can't ask to be forgiven of something we've done wrong if we have refused to forgive someone else of a wrong doing. Remember, sin is the only thing separates us from God. (Matthew 6:14-15 "If you forgive those who sin against you, your heavenly Father will forgive you. But if you refuse to forgive others, your Father will not forgive your sins.)

> If it is true that you look favorably on me, let me know your ways so I may understand you more fully and continue to enjoy your favor.
>
> *Exodus 13:33*

- **HATRED & REVENGE:** We can't enter into prayer with an attitude of hatred or revenge. We're supposed to pray for our enemies (and love them, too). (Matthew 5:43-48 "You have heard the law that says, 'Love your neighbor' and hate your enemy. But I say, love your enemies! Pray for those who persecute you! In that way, you will be acting as true children of your Father in heaven. For he gives his sunlight to both the evil and the good, and he sends rain on the just and the unjust alike. If

18

you love only those who love you, what reward is there for that? Even corrupt tax collectors do that much. If you are kind only to your friends, how are you different from anyone else? Even pagans do that. But you are to be perfect, even as your Father in heaven is perfect.")

- **VAIN REPETITION:** We're not supposed to just use vain repetition that is meaningless to us. (Matthew 6:7-8 "When you pray, don't babble on and on as people of other religions do. They think their prayers are answered merely by repeating their words again and again.")

- **STATUS:** We're not supposed to pray just for recognition. (Matthew 6:5 "When you pray, don't be like the hypocrites who love to pray publicly on street corners and in the synagogues where everyone can see them. I tell you the truth, that is all the reward they will ever get.")

- **RESPECT:** We shouldn't be irreverent or disrespectful. Even Jesus addressed God as "Holy Father" and "Righteous Father" in his prayers.

- **BELIEF:** We must work to come with an attitude of belief and faith. (Matthew 21:22 "You can pray for anything, and if you have faith, you will receive it.")

- **SUBMISSION:** We must make sure that our attitude is of submission. We cannot demand things from God but rather make humble requests. Once again, even Jesus exhibited this. (Matthew 26:29 "My Father, if it be possible, let this cup pass from me; nevertheless, not as I will, but as you will.")

- **GOD'S GREATER GLORY:** All we ask must be for the greater glory of God. There is no room for a selfish attitude in prayer. Jesus prayed not for his own comfort and well-being but for the glory of His father. (John 17:9

"My prayer is not for the world, but for those you have given me, because they belong to you.")

- **CONFIDENCE:** We are to pray with confidence. (I John 5:14-15 "And we are confident that he hears us whenever we ask for anything that pleases him. And since we know he hears us when we make our requests, we also know that he will give us what we ask for.")

- **PERSISTENCE:** We are to pray persistently. (Matthew 7:7-8 "Keep on asking, and you will receive what you ask for. Keep on seeking, and you will find. Keep on knocking, and the door will be opened to you. For everyone who asks, receives. Everyone who seeks, finds. And to everyone who knocks, the door will be opened.")

- **OBEDIENCE:** We must always strive for obedience. (I John 3:22 And we will receive from him whatever we ask because we obey him and do the things that please him.)

- **THANKSGIVING:** We must make our request with thanksgiving. (Philippians 4:6 Don't worry about anything; instead, pray about everything. Tell God what you need, and thank him for all he has done.)

THINK: Which attitude do you struggle with the most? Perhaps that is something to pray about...!

Why do I pray?

Because I
become a
different
person
when I pray
... and I like
the change.

4.   Prayer & Forgiveness

> **THINK:** What are some instances in your life that required someone to forgive you?

David's Prayer of Forgiveness

In I Samuel 13:14 David is described as a 'person after God's own heart.' As only a young man, he killed a giant and as an adult he was literally the stuff legends were made of. ("Saul has killed his thousands, and David his ten thousands! I Samuel 18:7) Yet, over the course of his life he became involved with a beautiful married woman and ended up committing adultery and finally, murder. David's prayer for forgiveness in Psalm 51 is in regard to his relationship with Bathsheba.

> *Have mercy on me, O God, because of your unfailing love. Because of your great compassion, blot out the stain of my sins.*
> *[2] Wash me clean from my guilt. Purify me from my sin.*
> *[3] For I recognize my rebellion; it haunts me day and night.*

22

⁴ Against you, and you alone, have I sinned; I have done what is evil in your sight. You will be proved right in what you say, and your judgment against me is just.

⁵ For I was born a sinner—yes, from the moment my mother conceived me.

⁶ But you desire honesty from the womb, teaching me wisdom even there.

⁷ Purify me from my sins, and I will be clean; wash me, and I will be whiter than snow.

⁸ Oh, give me back my joy again; you have broken me—now let me rejoice.

⁹ Don't keep looking at my sins. Remove the stain of my guilt.

¹⁰ Create in me a clean heart, O God. Renew a loyal spirit within me.

¹¹ Do not banish me from your presence, and don't take your Holy Spirit from me.

¹² Restore to me the joy of your salvation, and make me willing to obey you.

¹³ Then I will teach your ways to rebels, and they will return to you.

¹⁴ Forgive me for shedding blood, O God who saves, then I will joyfully sing of your forgiveness.

¹⁵ Unseal my lips, O Lord, that my mouth may praise you.

¹⁶ You do not desire a sacrifice, or I would offer one. You do not want a burnt offering.

¹⁷ The sacrifice you desire is a broken spirit. You will

not reject a broken and repentant heart, O God.
[18] Look with favor on Zion and help her; rebuild the
walls of Jerusalem.
[19] Then you will be pleased with sacrifices offered in
the right spirit—with burnt offerings and whole
burnt offerings. Then bulls will again be sacrificed
on your altar.

Securing forgiveness for our own sins is one thing, but what about forgiving others? D. L. Moody, an American evangelist and publisher, once said, "I firmly believe a great many prayers are not answered because we are not willing to forgive someone." The difficulty to forgive is not something new. Even the apostles struggled with forgiveness prompting Peter to ask Jesus in Matthew 18, "How often should I forgive someone who sins against me? Seven times?" Probably much to Peter's dismay, Jesus' response was, 'No, not seven times but seventy times seven!"

> Forget past failures, forget recurring sins, forget feelings of inferiority, and instead open your mind to God, who cannot fill what has not been emptied.
>
> *(Yancey, 185)*

Forgiveness is mentioned in the previous section regarding the proper attitude in prayer but it is such an important aspect of prayer that I felt it deserved its own section. The Bible is very definitive on forgiveness and our responsibility towards it: "If you forgive those who sin against you, your heavenly Father will forgive you. But if you refuse to forgive others, your Father will not forgive your sins." (Matthew 6:14-15)

But forgiveness is easier said than done, isn't it? I thought it important to give a few critical facts regarding forgiveness:

1. Forgiveness is an act of will not a feeling. It is a sign of strength not a show of weakness.

2. Forgiveness and reconciliation are not the same thing. Forgiveness only needs one person; reconciliation needs two.

3. Forgiveness is not a natural response but a supernatural response empowered by God.

4. Forgiveness is not based on what is fair but what is right and obedient to do.

5. Forgiveness is not based on waiting for time to heal wounds. Some wounds never heal.

6. Forgiveness is not ignoring hurt and anger but giving the hurt and anger to God.

7. Forgiveness is not forgetting but not keeping any active record of unjust behavior.

8. Forgiveness is not excusing or cancelling out consequences but merely allowing God to handle things in God's own way.

9. Forgiveness can be one of the most powerful points of witness for nonbelievers.

10. Forgiveness is a duty for all believers. (Luke 6:37 Do not judge others, and you will not be judged. Do not condemn others, or it will all come back against you. Forgive others, and you will be forgiven.)

Forgiveness is the ultimate expression of godly love. God loves us and has enabled our sins to be forgiven through the sacrifice of Jesus Christ. We must do the same. (Jeremiah 31:34b I will forgive their wickedness and I will never again remember their sins.)

THINK: Who needs your forgiveness?

Why do I pray?

Prayer invites God into my world and ushers me into God's.

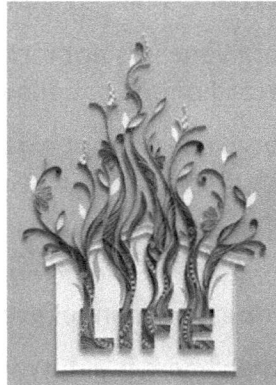

5. Prayer & The Right Kind of Requests

> **THINK:** If the promise in Matthew 7:7 which states, "Keep on asking, and you will receive what you ask for" is true, how come so many of our prayers go "unanswered"?

Do you ever tell your children, 'no'? Even if they really, *really* (please oh please oh please) wanted something? Even if they made earnest promises (I'll never ask for another thing again and I promise to do the dishes for a month)? Even if they had passionate, viable reasons for the request? (Everyone else is doing it and it will be so good for my self-confidence!) Even if they shed tears (You don't understand how important this is to me!)? My experience in being a parent is that it is easy to be a bad parent; it's unbelievably tough to be a good one. We say no to our children in our earnest attempt to *do what's right* for them in the long run even if they hate us at times in the interim. And still, even with our best intentions, because we are not perfect, we sometimes get it very wrong.

27

God's love for us and desire for us to be the best that we can be involves saying no to some of our most earnest requests. Thankfully, blessedly God *is* perfect and God *never* gets it wrong. We must remember that whenever we make a request.

> Just because He doesn't answer doesn't mean he don't care. Some of God's greatest gifts are unanswered prayers.
>
> (Yancey, 230)

In addition, we must remember what our purpose in life is: to be obedient to God and to fulfill our purpose which is to tell others about God. Our requests should *always* be to God's ultimate glory, our needs should *always* be for the accomplishment of God's perfect plan, our confidence should *always* rest on God's boundless love, and the answers to our prayers should *always* be defined by God's faultless wisdom.

Habakkuk's Honest Prayers

Habakkuk was a prophet of the Old Testament and wrote the Old Testament book that bears his name. He lived during a time when the Kingdom of Judah was threatened by outside enemies (the Babylonians would completely conquer them in less than 50 years) as well as inside enemies (most of Judah's kings were condemned by God for their wickedness). Habakkuk knew full well that his people faced a bleak future.

Habakkuk was unique among the prophets in that he openly questioned the way God worked. Yet even in his despair and worry he recognized who God was: His salvation, his strength, and his only hope for victory. His honest conversation is as pertinent today as it was when it was written in about 620 B.C.

> *How long, O Lord, must I call for help? But you do not listen!*
> *"Violence is everywhere!" I cry, but you do not come to save.*
> *3 Must I forever see these evil deeds? Why must I watch all this misery?*
> *Wherever I look, I see destruction and violence.*
> *I am surrounded by people who love to argue and fight.*
> *4 The law has become paralyzed, and there is no justice in the courts.*
> *The wicked far outnumber the righteous, so that justice has become perverted.*
>
> *Habakkuk 1:2-4*

> *I will climb up to my watchtower and stand at my guardpost. There I will wait to see what the Lord says and how he will answer my complaint.*
>
> *Habakkuk 2:1*

> *² I have heard all about you, LORD. I am filled with awe by your amazing works. In this time of our deep need, help us again as you did in years gone by. And in your anger, remember your mercy.*
>
> *Habakkuk 3:1-2*

[17] *Even though the fig trees have no blossoms, and there are no grapes on the vines;*
even though the olive crop fails, and the fields lie empty and barren; even though the flocks die in the fields, and the cattle barns are empty,
[18] *yet I will rejoice in the LORD! I will be joyful in the God of my salvation!*
[19] *The Sovereign LORD is my strength! He makes me as surefooted as a deer, able to tread upon the heights.*

Habakkuk 3:17-19

The Asking Attitude

Surely, indeed, truly, please allow this to be so.

My prayers are often filled with my worries, my needs, and my specific requests. Prayers like that have an inward perspective and focus merely on myself.

When Jesus prayed he rarely spoke of his personal needs but instead always cast his prayers *outward* looking at the world as a vast landscape in which he was to make a difference. In the famous Lord's Prayer (which we will discuss in depth in later) Jesus focused on the following things:

1. **Jesus Acknowledged** the might and power of God as well as our humble place.

2. **Jesus Honored** the supremacy of God.

3. **Jesus Desired** to be part of God's plan and purpose.

4. **Jesus Trusted** that God would provide everything needed.

5. **Jesus Asked** for forgiveness from God in the same way we are to forgive others on earth.

6. **Jesus Asked** for strength and wisdom to recognize and resist all evil.

7. **Jesus Surrendered** himself to God's Will, God's Direction, and God's Plan for his life.

What truths did Jesus speak of? How would your daily attitude change if you started each day by acknowledging God's might, power and supremacy?

What did Jesus desire? How would your life focus change if your only desire was to part of God's plan and purpose here on earth?

What were the only things that Jesus asked for? How much would your prayers change if your only formal requests were for forgiveness, strength, and wisdom?

In what did Jesus trust? How significant is an life outlook that knows that God provides all we need and has surrendered completely to God's Will, Direction and Specific Plans?

We all end our prayers with the word "Amen." Do you know what it means? It means any one of these translations:

- Surely/indeed/truly,
- Please allow this to be so, or
- We declare that we truly believe that God has heard everything we have said and that He will do it.

The more and more I think about prayer, the more and more it seems to almost be a 'verbal letter' to God. Take a look:

Your Prayer Envelope

- Who is this prayer from? Who are you in God's Eyes?
- Where is this prayer going? How do you view God?

FROM:

TO:

Your Prayer Letter

Your Salutation (Acknowledgement)

God is the Supreme Authority in both heaven and earth.

- *How will you address God?*

Your Opening (Honor/Thanks/Appreciation)

God has more influence and power over you and your life than anyone else and literally every good thing in your life has come from God.

- *What do you have in your life to be thankful and appreciative towards God?*

Your Promise (Commitment Reiterated)

God honors your personal freedom and choices and will never, ever force you to do anything.

God wants you to have a life filled with joy, peace, love, and fulfillment.

- *To what extent are you willing to be a part of God's plan for your life?*

Your Confession (Failures Acknowledged)

God desires a personal, intimate, life-long relationship with you and has gone to great lengths to make this possible. As a result, God has given you extensive directions as to how to be the best person God knows you can be.

God knows everything about you. God expects you to be exemplary to others who do not know of Him.

- *How have you not met the expectations and opportunities that God has provided to you?*

Your Requests (Needs Presented)

God has promised to never leave you, never lie to you, always defend you, and always cause everything to work out to the good if you trust in Him.

- *How can God enable you to be more powerful, more capable, and more exemplary to others who do not know of Him?*

Your Surrender (Submission Stated)

God has a reputation of being perfectly fair, perfectly loving, and perfectly forgiving.

God's ways are flawless.

- *What does God need to help you know, see, and understand in order to make you more useful?*

Your Closing (Final Words)

Surely, indeed, truly, please allow this to be so.

I declare that I truly believe that God has heard everything I have said and that He will do as He has promised.

- *How will you close your letter to God?*

The next time you pray, think about "Your Prayer Letter" in an attempt to help your prayers develop more meaning.

The Answering Attitude

There are three ways that God answers prayers: Yes, No, and Not Now.

Do you believe that God answers all prayers? From my way of thinking, prayers said by a believer are always answered by God. I john 5:14-15 states, "This is the confidence we have in approaching God that if we ask anything according to His will, He hears us. And if we know that He hears us—whatever we ask—we know that we have what we asked of Him." Prayers asked with the right attitude most certainly are answered because Jesus repeatedly promised that they would be:

- Matthew 7:7
- Matthew 18:19
- Matthew 21:22
- Mark 11:24
- Luke 11:13
- John 14:13-14
- John 16:23

Yet many regularly struggle with [what they believe to be] unanswered prayer requests. When we are faced with this situation, we must remember these things:

- God in His infinite wisdom knows what is best. We should never want something different than what God wants. Always remember that God can see all; not just the limited scope of we see.

- God is His infinite existence does not work within our timeframe; His timeframe is perfect. Patience is one of the most difficult skills a person can learn. Regarding God's timing, it is always worth the wait.

- This earthly life is not the ultimate goal and never should be. Our perspective must always be heavenward not earthbound.

- God is like the perfect parent wanting only the best for us but allowing to make our own choices and decisions *and mistakes.* It's called free will. Our ability to listen to God – or not – is a privilege only humans and angels have and with that privilege comes the burden of consequences as well.

THINK: Are you angry at God for 'unanswered' prayers in your life? How do these prayers compare to the style of your Prayer Letter To God? Have you talked to God about your feelings? Have you asked Him to help you understand the reasons for why He answered your prayer the way He did?

Why do I pray?

I pray because it's a way of saying, "**God show me what you are doing today and how I can be a part of it.**" I certainly have nothing better to do than to put myself in the stream of God's healing work on earth.

6. Prayer & The Holy Spirit

THINK: How do you rely on the Holy Spirit's in your daily walk?

Job's Prayer of Repentance

Many people know the story of Job. He was such a good man that God actually bragged about him to Satan. Satan's response was, in essence, 'The only reason Job respects you is because you've taken such good care of him. Things would surely change if you took away all you have given him!' Job's misery is recorded – the loss of his wife, children, wealth, and health – as well as his gradual questioning of just about everything he thought he understood. Yet through it all, Job never lost his reverence for his Lord. (Job 42:1-6)

> *Then Job replied to the LORD:*

2 "I know that you can do anything, and no one can stop you.

3 You asked, 'Who is this that questions my wisdom with such ignorance?' It is I—and I was talking about things I knew nothing about, things far too wonderful for me.

4 You said, 'Listen and I will speak! I have some questions for you, and you must answer them.'

5 I had only heard about you before, but now I have seen you with my own eyes.

6 I take back everything I said, and I sit in dust and ashes to show my repentance."

The original title of this section was "Prayer & My Shortcomings" but then I got thinking that God, in His infinite wisdom, already put things in place such that it is impossible for believers to have shortcomings when it involves prayer! You see, believers have the presence of the Holy Spirit with them at all times and in Romans 8:26 it clearly states, "And the Holy Spirit helps us in our weakness. For example, we don't know what God wants us to pray for. But the Holy Spirit prays for us with groanings that cannot be expressed in words."

In the busy chaos of our lives we tend to forget this wonderful presence that is with us at all times helping,

> We do far better to act like a trusting child, presenting foolish requests and letting the Father make judgments, than to fret in advance over appropriate petitions.
>
> *(Yancey, 320)*

39

encouraging, guiding, and comforting. Our human condition must rely on the power, might, and grace of the Holy Spirit to help us become more and more like the person God desires us to be. Through prayer, we open the communication channel in which God can work through us to accomplish mighty things. Through the Holy Spirit, our prayers, that key component in our relationship with God, are transformed into the ideal expressions that God needs to hear from us and we need to learn from Him.

My Failures

I have all these good intentions and yet I still keep getting it wrong.

If I get discouraged with myself, how must God feel about me? Paul knew exactly how you felt and wrote about it in Romans 7:18-24: "I want to do what is right, but I can't. I want to do what is good, but I don't. I don't want to do what is wrong, but I do it anyway. But if I do what I don't want to do, I am not really the one doing wrong; it is sin living in me that does it. I have discovered this principle of life—that when I want to do what is right, I inevitably do what is wrong. I love God's law with all my heart. But there is another power within me that is at war with my mind. This power makes me a slave to the sin that is still within me. Oh, what a miserable person I am!"

The great King David was another believer who regularly failed and sinned yet God called him in I Samuel 13:14 "a man after God's own heart." God *knows* our weaknesses and our struggles and this is where the *relationship* with God is so important. God didn't call David a man after his own heart because David got it right all the time; God called David a man after his own heart because David *never gave up trying to get it right* and *never gave up asking for forgiveness when he failed.*

Our relationship with God through our prayers – where we are honest with our emotions and our struggles in which we succeed *and fail* is the most loving, most forgiving, most empowering relationship we could ever hope to find in our lives. Prayer is the best way to deal with our failures – to ask for wisdom, strength, encouragement, and forgiveness.

My Poor Attitude

I can't always manage a good prayer attitude. Should I just not bother praying?

Okay, I'm completely intimidated now, regarding prayer. I'll never get the right attitude. I'll never be able to manage the right kind of request. Plus, already God knows what's in my heart. He's got to know that I'm … miserably, hopelessly only human.

In Mark 9 there is an account of a demon possessed boy who even the apostles couldn't heal. The father was told by Jesus that everything – even the healing of the little boy – was possible for one who believes. The father's heartfelt honest gave a beautiful picture of his belief and his sincerity. "I do believe," he told Jesus, "help me overcome my unbelief!" Every believer struggles with weak moments in their faith; it is part of the human condition and once again the Holy Spirit is always present to help up. It is important to note that after Jesus healed the little boy the apostles asked, "Why couldn't we drive out the demon?" Jesus' response? "This kind can come out *only by prayer.*" The apostles had become some confident with their God-given power and authority that they had *forgotten* to pray! Oops.

In other words, we are to do *our level best* and even when that's lacking, God's provided us with the Holy Spirit to make sure everything is appropriate.

When we just can't manage the proper attitudes and words for God in prayer, perhaps that is the perfect time to simply bow our heads, quiet our thoughts, and just strive to listen to God's comforting words and presence.

My Doubts & Fears

Maybe I shouldn't say this but what if God's Will isn't what I want?
I wish I could be the wonderful, wise Christian who never worries, never doubts, and always faces every crisis with confidence knowing that God Is In Control Of Everything. But I'm not perfect and mess up all the time and that's just the reality of who I am. Even praying for God's Will can be terrifying for me because it might be so very far from where I am and where I think I need to be.

How do you view God? Is God an avenging being sitting up in heaven waiting to throw a thunderbolt at you when you get things wrong? Is [your impression of] God's primary purpose to love or to punish us? Encourage or to control us? Guide or to force us? The Bible tells us that God's primary emotion is love. I John 4:8 says, "But anyone who does not love does not know God, for God is love." And not only does God love, God loves *unconditionally.* Paul describes the kind of love that God has this way in I Corinthians 13:4-7: "Love is patient and kind. Love is not jealous or boastful or proud or rude. It does not demand its own way. It is not irritable, and it keeps no record of being wronged. It

42

does not rejoice about injustice but rejoices whenever the truth wins out. Love never gives up, never loses faith, is always hopeful, and endures through every circumstance."

A God who loves like that only wants the best for you: love, joy, peace, patience, kindness, goodness, faithfulness, gentleness, and self-control (Galatians 5:22-23). These things are called *the fruits of the Spirit;* these things are the benefit of the Holy Spirit's presence in our lives. Don't you want to jump on the boat and never get off?

Our faith is something that changes (and hopefully grows) daily with the help of the Holy Spirit. The Bible likens us to starting out as babies capable of only consuming baby food and we are charged with eventually working our way up to meals of steak and wine. Paul wrote in I Corinthians 3:1-2, "Dear brothers and sisters, when I was with you I couldn't talk to you as I would to spiritual people. I had to talk as though you belonged to this world or as though you were infants in the Christian life. I had to feed you with milk, not with solid food, because you weren't ready for anything stronger." Jesus said it a different way in Luke 16:10, "If you are faithful in little things, you will be faithful in large ones." Both passages seek to get you to understand a critical fact about faith: it's got to be ever-present in *all areas of your life* for you to reap those wonderfully promised rewards. Practice makes perfect is applicable to your prayer life: the more you do it, the more capable you become. If your prayer life only roars to life when crises hit, you will never receive the full benefit of a vibrant relationship with Jesus Christ.

How do you envision God? What kind of friendship do you have with God? Are you just a fat baby? How are you with the little things in your life will directly impact how you are with the big things in your life. With the Holy Spirit's guiding influence, our shortcomings actually become potential areas of greatest strength. Remember what 2 Corinthians 12:9 says, "My grace is all you need. My power works best in weakness."

THINK: Don't ever be afraid to pray for yourself: your struggles, your doubts, and your fears. Where is your greatest shortcoming when it comes to prayer? Have you prayed about it?

Why do I pray?

Prayer does not fit us for the greater work; prayer is the greater work.
Oswald Chambers

7. Prayer & God's Will

> **THINK:** What are some of the arguments you know against praying and relying on God? Do you have responses to these arguments?

Jonah Prayer From Inside The Fish

God spoke to Jonah and gave him a message that he was to   •
deliver to the people of the city of Ninevah. Jonah promptly got
up and went ... in the opposite direction, which is why he ended
up in the belly of a fish with plenty of time to consider his blatant
disobedience to God. The Bible says that God talks to us with a
still, small voice but sometimes we need a slightly *louder*
communication. Jonah's prayer, from the belly of the fish, is
beautiful in its acknowledgement of the truth. When we pray, we

need to remember that God already knows the truth ... we just have to admit it. (Jonah 2:1-9)

> *Then Jonah prayed to the LORD his God from inside the fish. [2] He said,*
>
> *"I cried out to the LORD in my great trouble, and he answered me. I called to you from the land of the dead, and LORD, you heard me!*
> *[3] You threw me into the ocean depths, and I sank down to the heart of the sea.*
> *The mighty waters engulfed me; I was buried beneath your wild and stormy waves.*
> *[4] Then I said, 'O LORD, you have driven me from your presence. Yet I will look once more toward your holy Temple.'*
>
> *[5] "I sank beneath the waves, and the waters closed over me. Seaweed wrapped itself around my head.*
> *[6] I sank down to the very roots of the mountains. I was imprisoned in the earth, whose gates lock shut forever. But you, O LORD my God, snatched me from the jaws of death!*
> *[7] As my life was slipping away, I remembered the LORD. And my earnest prayer went out to you in your holy Temple.*
> *[8] Those who worship false gods turn their backs on all God's mercies.*
> *[9] But I will offer sacrifices to you with songs of praise, and I will fulfill all my vows. For my salvation comes from the LORD alone."*

Why did Jonah disobey? Did he doubt himself? Did he doubt God? Nothing is harder than dealing with doubt – whether it is your own or someone else's which has been directed at you. Being obedient to God, following God's plan for our life regularly puts us in situations that might cause us to doubt or fear. But trusting in God and achieving successes in situations that are beyond our comfort zone is the best and quickest way to grow spiritually.

And don't worry about your history. Forget about your failures. Always remember that *your personal story* is the *only thing* that others cannot argue with because *it's yours.* Don't worry about remembering scripture or what your pastor or your Bible study teacher has said, instead *speak from your heart* when you are faced with doubters. Nothing is more authentic and more powerful than honest, heartfelt accounts of how the Lord has worked in your life and what you have experienced personally.

Let's look at a few good questions regarding prayer and God's Will.

Why Bother?

God knows how everything will happen, why does He need me to pray about it?

It's a good question and if we asked a hundred people we'd probably get a hundred different answers. Here are a few good reasons why we should pray:

1. **Because we are told to**. We are called to be obedient. The Old Testament is filled with God's chosen people being told to do one thing to ensure God's care and guidance and them doing exactly the opposite with dire

consequences. Do not behave like a disobedient child. Jeremiah 42:3 Pray that the Lord your God will tell us where we should go and what we should do. Luke 18:1 One day Jesus told his disciples a story to show that they should always pray and never give up.

2. **Because Jesus did.** If it's good enough for Jesus it must certainly be good enough for us. Read Jesus' final prayer in the Garden of Gethsemane just before he was arrested. Take special note of who and what he prayed for. Then take note of how many of Jesus' requests were answered. You might be surprised at what you discover.

3. **Because it is the best way to know God's Will and gain spiritual wisdom.** How else is God supposed to communicate with you? Comfort you? Guide you? If you are worried, confused, or frightened, prayer is the best way to seek and learn God's advice and wisdom. Colossians 1:9 So we have not stopped praying for you since we first heard about you. We ask God to give you complete knowledge of his will and to give you spiritual wisdom and understanding.

> I remind myself that the Son of God, who had spoken worlds into being and sustains all that exists, felt a compelling need to pray. He prayed as if it made a difference, as if the time he devoted to prayer mattered every bit as much as the time he devoted to caring for people.
>
> *(Yancey, 79)*

4. **Because it changes me in a good way.** Prayer doesn't change things it changes us and then we change things around us. Prayer enlightens our minds with God's Truth. Romans 12:2 Don't copy the behavior and customs of this world, but let God transform you into a new person by changing the way you think. Then you will learn to know God's will for you, which is good and pleasing and perfect.

Hasn't God Already Decided?

What difference can my prayers make?

God has *always* operated in tangent with humans. Adam in the garden; Noah and the flood, Deborah and Barak, Mary and Joseph ... Each of us have a purpose; each of us are called to further God's kingdom on earth. God *works* with humans and our prayers enable us to become a part of God's plan on earth. James 5:16b states, "The earnest prayer of a righteous person has great power and produces wonderful results." That sounds like a difference to me.

The important thing to remember is that we are not praying to change God's mind or inform God of something He may know or not know. We are praying so that we can become a part of God's changing power on earth and when that happens *we're changing* in a good way. Remember, God might know everything, but we don't. We need to stay in constant communication with God to stay in tune with His plans.

Why Should I Trust God?

Where are you headed?

A key component of belief is trust. What is your ultimate goal in life? What is your 'final reward'? Do you believe in heaven? If you do, are you confident you're going to heaven? You should have answers for these questions. Jesus said, "For God loved the world so much that he gave his one and only Son, so that everyone who believes in him will not perish but have eternal life. God sent his Son into the world not to judge the world, but to save the world through him."

Do you believe that God loves us, cares for us, and only wants the best for us? Do you believe these following verses?

- Psalm 23:1 The Lord is my shepherd, I shall not want.
- Psalm 115:12 The Lord has been mindful of us; He will bless us.
- Matthew 10:30-31 But the very hairs of your head are all numbered. So do not fear; you are more valuable than many sparrows.
- Psalm 103:13 Just as a father has compassion on his children, so the Lord has compassion on those who fear Him.
- Deuteronomy 31:6 Be strong and courageous. Do not be afraid or terrified because of them, for the Lord you God goes with you; he will never leave you nor forsake you.

Your level of trust in God's promises will directly impact how you view a life dictated by God's Will … or not. *It is essential that you decide;* not making a firm decision *is* a decision. Regarding indecision regarding belief or not the Bible says, "Since you are like lukewarm water, neither hot nor cold, I will spit you out of my mouth!" (Revelations 3:16)

A key component of belief is trust in God's promises and this will directly impact your prayer life attitude ... and success.

> **THINK:** What are some things in the past that you wanted <u>desperately</u> but did not come about despite your earnest prayers? Given the passage of time and the changes in your life now, can you see the reason why God led you in a different direction?

Why do I pray?

Prayer is like fuel. Without, I get nowhere.

Prayer & God

Prayer, Posture, & Style

Prayer & the Proper Attitude

Prayer & Forgiveness

Prayer & The Right Kind of Requests

Prayer & The Holy Spirit

Prayer & God's Will

8.   Prayer & Power

> **THINK:** How often do you limit yourself based on your lack of
> faith in God's power and might?

Hezekiah's Prayer On His Deathbed

Poor King Hezekiah. Lying sick in bed, God's prophet Isaiah visits
him and says, "Set your affairs in order, for you are going to die.
You will not recover from this illness." Hezekiah was one of a very
few kings who 'did what was pleasing in the Lord's sight'. For
twenty-nine years he 'remained faithful to the Lord in everything,
carefully obeying all the commands that the Lord had given
Moses.' (2 Kings 18) Yet, Isaiah's news, devastated him causing
him to curl un and … pray. (Isaiah 38:2-8)

[2] *When Hezekiah heard this, he turned his face to the wall and prayed to the LORD,* *[3]* *"Remember, O LORD, how I have always been faithful to you and have served you single-mindedly, always doing what pleases you." Then he broke down and wept bitterly.*

[4] *Then this message came to Isaiah from the LORD:* *[5]* *"Go back to Hezekiah and tell him, 'This is what the LORD, the God of your ancestor David, says: I have heard your prayer and seen your tears. I will add fifteen years to your life,* *[6]* *and I will rescue you and this city from the king of Assyria. Yes, I will defend this city.*

[7] *"'And this is the sign from the LORD to prove that he will do as he promised:* *[8]* *I will cause the sun's shadow to move ten steps backward on the sundial of Ahaz!'" So the shadow on the sundial moved backward ten steps.*

Our honest prayers and our purpose in this life are of vital importance to God. Never forget that.

The greatest limitation on the power of God in this world is *us*. Instead of that being a condemnation, let it become a battle cry. (Just take a look at how God answered Hezekiah's prayer in Isaiah 38:4-7.) A verse that is particularly precious to me is Ephesians 3:20 which says, "Now all glory to God, who is able, through His mighty power at work within us, to accomplish infinitely more than we might ask or think." Praying with the right attitude and the right goals in mind unleashes the same power that raised Jesus Christ from the dead!

Infinitely more than we might ask or think. Consider the implications of that statement!

Miracles

Any limitations come only from our side.

The definition of coincidence is a remarkable concurrence of events or circumstances without apparent causal connection. The definition of miracle is a surprising and welcome event that is not explicable by natural or scientific laws and is therefore considered to be the work of a divine agency. Personally, I don't think there is such a thing as coincidence. If God is involved in all aspects of our lives than that must mean that nothing is left to chance but instead left to our obedience to God's direction and the consequences of those decisions. I love the saying "coincidence is God's way of remaining anonymous." Limitations we place on the scope and magnitude of our prayers come only from us. Ephesians 1:19-20 tells us, "I also pray that you will understand the incredible greatness of God's power for us who believe him. This is the same mighty power that raised Christ from the dead and seated him in the place of honor at God's right hand in the heavenly realms."

> We would accomplish more for the world by praying faithfully than by walking into the White House, or Whitehall, or the Kremlin with suggestions.
>
> *(Yancey 309)*

On the flip side, please remember that any miracle recorded in the Bible as well as any miracle that has occurred since has always and only been expressly for God's great glory and the furtherance of His plan here on earth. After all, that's what this life is all about.

Personal Strength & Confidence

When we pray, God works.
Prayers have a tremendous impact, particularly on a believer's faith and life.

- **Prayer gives access to power** that will help stand the test of all manner of storms. (Psalm 50:15 Call upon me in the day of trouble; I shall rescue you, and you will honor Me.)

- **Prayer helps us stand against temptations** that we face daily. (Matthew 26:41: Watch and pray that you may not enter into temptation. The spirit indeed is willing, but the flesh is weak.)

- **Prayer brings about positive godly changes** to the lives of those around us. (I Timothy 2:1-4 I urge that supplications, prayers, intercessions, and thanksgivings be made for all people, for kings and all who are in high positions, that we may lead a peaceful and quiet life, godly and dignified in every way. This is good, and it is pleasing in the sight of God our Savior, who desires all people to be saved and to come to the knowledge of the truth.)

Defense & Care

I have had hard times in my life, times of fear and hurt, anger and despair. I don't think there is anyone who hasn't had difficulties in life. In fact, the older I get the more I realize that traveling from one hardship to the other is essentially the reality of the human existence.

God knows this. I believe that this was part of God's grief and anger when sin first entered into the world; God knew how tough it was going to be for us. The power of prayer is God's defensive shield for us. Prayer is Satan's kryptonite and our secret weapon. Believing in the power of prayer and trusting in God's promises of care for us are all we need to do.

Here are just a few verses that talk about God's care for us; He is only just a prayer away.

- Ask me and I will tell you remarkable secrets you do not know about things to come. Jeremiah 33:3

- Fear not, for I am with you; be not dismayed, for I am your God; I will strengthen you, I will help you, I will uphold you with my righteous right hand. Isaiah 41:10

- God is our refuge and strength, a very present help in trouble. Psalm 46:1

- The Lord will rescue me from every evil deed and bring me safely into his heavenly kingdom. 2 Timothy 4:18

- Though I walk in the midst of trouble, you preserve my life; you stretch out your hand against the wrath of my enemies and your right hand delivers me. Psalm 138:7 NIV

THINK: What are some 'impossible' things in your life that you should be praying about?

Why do I pray?

Because
prayer
makes me
feel
mighty.

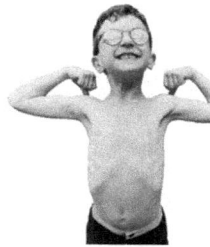

9.   Prayer & Hardships

THINK: How do you deal with hardships in your life?

Jehoshaphat's Prayer for Deliverance

Jehoshaphat was the fourth king of the Kingdom of Judah. In general, he did what was pleasing to the Lord although he did not remove all the pagan shrines that were throughout the land. (I Kings 22:43) When he learned that a vast army was marching against he, he was terrified and prayed to the Lord for guidance. (2 Chronicles 20:5-12)

> *⁵ Jehoshaphat stood before the community of Judah and Jerusalem in front of the new courtyard at the*

58

*Temple of the L*ORD*. ⁶ He prayed, "O L*ORD*, God of our ancestors, you alone are the God who is in heaven. You are ruler of all the kingdoms of the earth. You are powerful and mighty; no one can stand against you! ⁷ O our God, did you not drive out those who lived in this land when your people Israel arrived? And did you not give this land forever to the descendants of your friend Abraham? ⁸ Your people settled here and built this Temple to honor your name. ⁹ They said, 'Whenever we are faced with any calamity such as war, plague, or famine, we can come to stand in your presence before this Temple where your name is honored. We can cry out to you to save us, and you will hear us and rescue us.'*

¹⁰ "And now see what the armies of Ammon, Moab, and Mount Seir are doing. You would not let our ancestors invade those nations when Israel left Egypt, so they went around them and did not destroy them. ¹¹ Now see how they reward us! For they have come to throw us out of your land, which you gave us as an inheritance. ¹² O our God, won't you stop them? We are powerless against this mighty army that is about to attack us. We do not know what to do, but we are looking to you for help."

How God answered Jehoshaphat's prayer is exciting and unexpected! (Check it out: 2 Chronicles 20:13-30.) Everyone reacts differently when hardships come our way. Some of us need to share our worries with others, sort of like spreading out the load so that it's easier to carry. Others of us prefer to keep the entire responsibility of the problem all to ourselves as long as we can. When we finally do reach out, those of us who have the privilege of having close friends or family members always head in that direction first. Having someone who can offer a shoulder to cry on, a sympathetic ear that's willing to listen, and wise words of advice that offer suggestions can mean the world.

> Remember that God also buried his Son on the mission field.
>
> *(Yancey, 231)*

God wants you to communicate with Him when you are happy as well as when you are sad. Major portions of the Old Testament deal with human beings who face all manner of trials and how God helped them survive and even thrive. Look at some of these verses:

- Isaiah 41:10 Don't be afraid, for I am with you. Don't be discouraged, for I am your God. I will strengthen you and help you. I will hold you up with my victorious right hand.

- John 16:33 I have told you all this so that you may have peace in me. Here on earth you will have many trials and sorrows. But take heart, because I have overcome the world.

- Romans 8:28 And we know that God causes everything to work together for the good of those who love God and are called according to his purpose for them.

- Philippians 4:6 "Don't worry about anything; instead, pray about everything. Tell God what you need, and thank him for all he has done."

Whether you are the type of person who likes to share your worries with others or keep them all to yourself, you *must* make a conscious decision to bring them to the Lord in prayer.

In addition, those who have an active, vital prayer life will never be caught unawares when hardships arise; they will have already established a firm foundation with a prayerful relationship with God.

"Everything to work together for good..."

We cannot stand in the shoes of God and give an answer to questions that ask "Why?" regarding tragedies and "unanswered prayers. We don't have God's mind and don't see with God's eyes." We simply cannot understand everything with a finite perspective. Even the Bible speaks of this in I Corinthians 13:12, "Now we see things imperfectly, like puzzling reflections in a mirror, but then we will see everything with perfect clarity. All that I know now is partial and incomplete, but then I will know everything completely, just as God now knows me completely." Trying to understand why there is suffering and tragedy in our lives and in our world is just something that we cannot do at this time. What we must remember is this world is not perfect, our bodies are not perfect, and we are not perfect. Imperfection – evil – is in our world and where sorrow and tragedy comes from. But we can know that God's ultimate emotion is love; it is the highest value in the universe.

Free will was a gift given to humans (and the angels); the ability to choose to love or not to love. With free will comes the ability to reject God. The opposite of God's goodness is evil. Much of the world's suffering results from the sinful action or inaction of ourselves and others. Our hand can be used for goodness or for evil; it's our choice. God didn't create evil but He did allow the potential for evil so that we could have the opportunity for goodness and love. It's a little like choosing to become parents; many of us choose to do it simply because of the potential for joy even though the potential for heartache is always there, too.

No one has a charmed life. No. One. We all endure our own sorrows. There is a promise that is very important to me, especially during times of hardship and grief. I have clung to it through the worst times of my life. It says, "And we know that God causes everything to work together for the good of those who love God and are called according to his purpose for them." (Romans 8:28) That promise that even in the darkness moments of life God promises to work for the good means more to me than I can adequately express. It means that nothing is out of God's realm of care or concern for me and that I am never alone.

THINK: In the midst of a hardship, can you see evidence of God's love and care? What has God put into place *in anticipation* of this difficult event in your life?

Why do I pray?

Prayer
keeps
me
calm.

62

10. Prayer & Me

THINK: What is your #1 prayer request regarding yourself? Were God to say 'yes' to this request, how would it further God's plans for this world?

Solomon's Prayer Request

Solomon was a prince. His father was King David and his mother was Bathsheba. The Bible specifically states that "The Lord loved him" and actually called him 'Jedidiah' which means 'beloved of the Lord'. (2 Samuel 12:25) When Solomon assumed the throne, God appeared to him in a dream and said, "Ask whatever you

wish, and I'll give it to you." (I Kings 3:5) You might be surprised
at what he asked for. (I Kings 3:5-10)

> [5] That night the LORD appeared to Solomon in a
> dream, and God said, "What do you want? Ask, and
> I will give it to you!"
>
> [6] Solomon replied, "You showed faithful love to your
> servant my father, David, because he was honest
> and true and faithful to you. And you have
> continued your faithful love to him today by giving
> him a son to sit on his throne.
>
> [7] "Now, O LORD my God, you have made me king
> instead of my father, David, but I am like a little
> child who doesn't know his way around. [8] And here
> I am in the midst of your own chosen people, a
> nation so great and numerous they cannot be
> counted! [9] Give me an understanding heart so that I
> can govern your people well and know the
> difference between right and wrong. For who by
> himself is able to govern this great people of
> yours?"
>
> [10] The Lord was pleased that Solomon had asked for
> wisdom.

Many of us pray as often as we can – in the car, in line at the
grocery, and while having a difficult conversation with a loved
one. That is wonderful and just what we are called to do. Yet we
should have formal, focused prayer time in our lives and this is
what I will address now.

Time & Location

Commit to finding a consistent place and time that is free from distractions; no phone, no television, no kids. Maybe it's your commute to work, or your workout time on the treadmill, or first thing in the morning. It's got to be something that works *for you*. Ask your friends what they do; maybe they'll have good suggestions.

Dialogue

Begin your conversation with God. Don't worry about posture or words or what style of prayer you're doing. Say it quietly or out loud with your eyes closed or open. *Just begin.*

- Start with things you're thankful for in your life. Can you name a new one each day? Think of your life, your circumstances, your job, your family, your friends, the world around you … "Whatever is good and perfect comes down to us from God our Father, who created all the lights in the heavens. He never changes or casts a shifting shadow." (James 1:17) These are blessings in your life. Have you ever formally thanked God for them?

- Apologize for all the times you have let God down whether through disobedience, inaction, misbehavior or ignorance. Ask Him to forgive you for all your sins and ask Him to help you become stronger, better, and wiser next time.

- Tell God your worries, your fears, and your struggles. Ask for insight, help, and solutions. Ask God to show you His Will for all the things that you are stressing about. I always pray for Big Black Arrows under the theory that I'm rather clueless and preoccupied much of the time so if God would just paint Big Black Arrows on the ground I'll be happy to follow them.

- Ask God what He needs for you to do. Tell Him you are His and willing to do whatever He needs you to do. Give yourself some quiet moments where you just let God speak to you. Do you think of someone you feel you should reach out to? Someone you need to forgive? Someone you need to reconnect with? Something someone has asked you to do that you originally declined? Someone who needs your assistance?

Prayer is a personal exercise and I do not want to give you so many specifics that your prayers become mine. However these are a few things that I do that I find great satisfaction in doing:

- I like to write in a journal and keep track of my praises and my prayer requests. It is fun to see how often my prayer requests become my praises. It is amazing to me to watch how God solves what seem to be my biggest problem in simple, unique, (sometimes humorous) ways.

> I like to think of my conversations with people as prayer ... I willingly refer my actions to God, and in doing so they become a prayer.
>
> *(Yancey, 314)*

- I sometimes use my prayer time to memorize scripture and there are times when I just say aloud what I have memorized instead of any other kind of praying. It can be a very emotional, powerful time!

- I sometimes wear a special bracelet or ring to help me remember to pray for a particular person. When I see it on my hand, it reminds me to say a quick prayer.

- I try to connect (call or email) with people that come to my mind during my prayers. I can't tell you how often that person is absolutely shocked that I called and said, "You came to my mind when I was praying today and I just wanted to know how you're doing." Often they are in crisis or need or just lonely and my connection was exactly what they needed.

- I have a collection of close spiritual friends that I call on when I need prayer for myself (and vice versa). When I start to really struggle (can't sleep, can't focus) because of worry that's my clue that I need others praying for me and my issues besides just myself. I can't tell you how many times I immediately feel better for doing this.

- I have a collection of close spiritual friends who know my deepest, darkest struggles and who pray for me regularly and I them.

- I am on the church prayer chain and get notification via email of praises and prayer requests. It keeps me connected to the church body and also allows me another place to request prayer for myself and my loved ones.

Do you have spiritual friends? Ask them how they approach prayer. What works for them and what doesn't? What suggestions do they have? How has prayer helped them? Sharing stories, techniques, successes and failures are all opportunities for growth and improvement in our prayer lives.

Listen & Obey

Coincidence has no place in your prayer life.
When you pray and something happens or someone speaks to you about exactly the issue that you were praying about or the minister preaches a sermon on exactly the topic you're struggling

with or someone offers you a solutions out of the clear blue never, *ever* attribute that to anything other than God's mighty power at work. Remember there are others out there praying for the Lord's Guidance, asking to be shown the Lord's Will and striving to do the thing that God is telling them; that's how God works!!

THINK: What is the single most important thing you can do for God in your life right now? Have you prayed about this?

Why do I pray?

Evidently, God likes to be asked.

11. Prayer & Others

> **THINK:** How does praying for others affect your relationship with them?

Jesus's Prayer At Gethsemane

The simplest answer to the question "Why pray?" is "Because Jesus did." (78) Jesus relied on prayer as a kind of spiritual recharging. (79)

What are some examples about what Jesus prayed for?

69

- CHILDREN Matthew 19:13-15

- FOOD Mark 6:41-44

- STRENGTH/FAILURES Luke 22:31-32

- EXAMPLE/APPRECIATION John 11:38-42

- PERSONAL ADVOCATE John 14:16-18

- UNITY OF BELIEVERS John 17:20-23

- UNITY/UNBELIEVERS/PROTECTION/EDUCATION/JOY John 17:6-19

Jesus knew the sensation of getting no answers to his pleas. (78) Prayer for trivial things ... had little place in Jesus' practice. (78) Jesus' prayers ... show a remarkable lack of concern about his own needs. (78)

Just before he would be arrested, tried and crucified, Jesus went to the Garden of Gethsemane and prays. John recorded the prayer in his Gospel, chapter 17. As you read this prayer, think about what we now know was to happen. Then take special note of what Jesus specifically prayed for.

> "Father, if you are willing, please take this cup of suffering away from me. Yet I want your will to be done, not mine."
>
> *Luke 22:42*

"Father, the hour has come. Glorify your Son so he can give glory back to you. [2] For you have given him authority over everyone. He gives eternal life to each one you have given him. [3] And this is the way to have eternal life—to know you, the only true God, and Jesus Christ, the one you sent to earth. [4] I

70

brought glory to you here on earth by completing the work you gave me to do. ⁵ Now, Father, bring me into the glory we shared before the world began.

⁶ "I have revealed you to the ones you gave me from this world. They were always yours. You gave them to me, and they have kept your word. ⁷ Now they know that everything I have is a gift from you, ⁸ for I have passed on to them the message you gave me. They accepted it and know that I came from you, and they believe you sent me.

⁹ "My prayer is not for the world, but for those you have given me, because they belong to you. ¹⁰ All who are mine belong to you, and you have given them to me, so they bring me glory. ¹¹ Now I am departing from the world; they are staying in this world, but I am coming to you. Holy Father, you have given me your name; now protect them by the power of your name so that they will be united just as we are. ¹² During my time here, I protected them by the power of the name you gave me. I guarded them so that not one was lost, except the one headed for destruction, as the Scriptures foretold.

¹³ "Now I am coming to you. I told them many things while I was with them in this world so they would be filled with my joy. ¹⁴ I have given them your word. And the world hates them because they do not belong to the world, just as I do not belong to the world. ¹⁵ I'm not asking you to take them out of the world, but to keep them safe from the evil one. [16] *They do not belong to this world any more than I do.* [17] *Make them holy by your truth; teach them your word, which is truth.* [18] *Just as you sent me into the world, I am sending them into the world.* [19] *And I give myself as a holy sacrifice for them so they can be made holy by your truth.*

[20] *"I am praying not only for these disciples but also for all who will ever believe in me through their message.* [21] *I pray that they will all be one, just as you and I are one—as you are in me, Father, and I am in you. And may they be in us so that the world will believe you sent me.*

[22] *"I have given them the glory you gave me, so they may be one as we are one.* [23] *I am in them and you are in me. May they experience such perfect unity that the world will know that you sent me and that you love them as much as you love me.* [24] *Father, I want these whom you have given me to be with me where I am. Then they can see all the glory you gave me because you loved me even before the world began!*

[25] *"O righteous Father, the world doesn't know you, but I do; and these disciples know you sent me.* [26] *I have revealed you to them, and I will continue to do so. Then your love for me will be in them, and I will be in them."*

Susan McGeown

I once had a boyfriend turn to me in the middle of the Superbowl and scream, "PRAY THAT THE GIANTS WIN!! HURRY!!!" Now I guess I could be pleased that 1.) He appreciated that I was a woman of prayer and 2.) He recognized the power and speed of prayers but at that moment in time I was horrified at his request. I'm fairly certain that sport and lottery wins are ranked rather low on quality prayers.

I have sobbed broken heartedly over a lost love and agonized over health issues of family and friends and even then I've always been careful of how I say my prayers. You see, I never, ever want to usurp God's Will or God's Plans for my life or any other person's life. When times are trying I always pray for wisdom, peace, guidance, strength, and comfort for all involved.

I remember when I was first married and the possibility of my husband being transferred loomed over my head. I panicked not wanting to leave my parents, my friends, my family, my church … My roots when very deep. My husband got upset, too, knowing how unhappy I was about the potential relocation. That made me realize that in addition to not wanting to move, I also didn't want to hinder my husband's progress in life either. What if this new job opportunity was God's will?

So I prayed, but I didn't ask to stay and I also didn't ask to go. I just remember praying tearfully, "Help!!" because I literally didn't know what else to do. And then I had an epiphany. It was bright and clear and so powerful that I immediately felt calm. I realized that I trusted God and believed that He only wanted what was the best for me. My life was proof of that so far wasn't it? And God would never move me to a place that was *less* than what I already had so then that would have to mean that wherever God would send me than it had to be as good or better than what I already had! Suddenly, I was peaceful and calm … and even a tiny bit excited … about the move. In the end, we never moved but I never forgot that blessed experience: the reality of God's love and care for me and mine.

My parents taught me how to pray like this and modeled it through the death of their child from a genetic illness. I remember sitting in church while the minister prayed for a miracle and wondering why God wasn't answering that prayer. My mom told me that she, too, prayed for healing but at some point in her prayers she 'just knew' that my sister was not going to be healed. Instead of giving up, Mom began to pray for time. The last five years of my sister's life my mother called her 'years of grace.' My sister died just before she turned twelve.

My point of this chapter is to encourage you to see God's Will in every aspect of your life, not just your own. Remember that in your prayer requests for others and trust that God is in control of it all.

THINK: Do you utilize other's prayers when you need strength and help?

Why do I pray?

Simply
put,
because
Jesus did.

Prayer & God

Prayer, Posture, & Style

Prayer & the Proper Attitude

Prayer & Forgiveness

Prayer & The Right Kind of Requests

Prayer & The Holy Spirit

Prayer & God's Will

Prayer & Power

Prayer & Hardships

Prayer & Me

Pray & Others

12. Prayer and God's Response

THINK: God's three responses to our prayers are "Yes," "No," and "Not right now."

Paul's Prayer For Spiritual Growth

Ephesus was one of the largest most important trade cities in Asia with a population of over 300,000 during Paul's ministry. Politically, commercially and religiously it was an advanced, cosmopolitan city that claimed wealth, prominence, and power. Culturally diverse, a visitor walking the city's streets would find Asians, Greeks, Persians, and Romans in abundance. One of its greatest structural wonders was the Temple of Diana with priests that also served as bankers for its treasure house and who oversaw the vast numbers of pilgrims that came from all over the world to not only worship the goddess Diana but visit the temple's museum and market place.

The church at Ephesus, that Paul had helped establish, struggled with this heavily idolatrous city and faced numerous struggles both inside and outside its walls such as false teachers, unfaithful people, and ethnic tensions between Jewish and Gentile Christians. In his letter to the church at Ephesus, Paul prayed for their spiritual growth. (Ephesians 3:14-21)

> [14] *When I think of all this, I fall to my knees and pray to the Father,* [15] *the Creator of everything in heaven and on earth.*
>
> [16] *I pray that from his glorious, unlimited resources he will empower you with inner strength through his Spirit.*
>
> [17] *Then Christ will make his home in your hearts as you trust in him. Your roots will grow down into God's love and keep you strong.*

18 And may you have the power to understand, as all God's people should, how wide, how long, how high, and how deep his love is.

19 May you experience the love of Christ, though it is too great to understand fully. Then you will be made complete with all the fullness of life and power that comes from God.

Many of Jesus' prayers remained still unanswered today.

20 Now all glory to God, who is able, through his mighty power at work within us, to accomplish infinitely more than we might ask or think.

21 Glory to him in the church and in Christ Jesus through all generations forever and ever! Amen.

Just because God doesn't answer our specific prayer doesn't mean that He is not present, not caring, and not actively working in our lives. Nor should we assume that God is ignoring us and our specific needs. We must, when we approach God in prayer, remember that God is the master potter and that we are just the clay pot He is shaping. God knows the entire picture, we only know the few brush strokes that touch our lives.

Think about this: some of God's greatest blessings are unanswered prayers! I'm speaking from my own experience – relations I desperately wanted to continue but failed, jobs I earnestly wanted to get but didn't, and opportunities I felt were the best way to go but ended unsuccessfully. I have learned to trust God in all situations – the good as well as the bad. I trust that God:

1. Knows best.

2. Is always present with me.

3. Is always actively involved in my life.

4. Has gone before me to prepare my path during difficult times.

5. Can make any situation into a victory in my life.

In addition, regarding my prayer requests, I always want God to

1. Take every prayer request I make and reshape it in a manner that will be the very best for His Kingdom.

2. Ignore my wants and needs if it means that God's Kingdom will be hindered or hurt in any way.

3. Help me to see His clear direction and wants.

4. Use me in the best way possible.

THINK: How can God use you best?

Why do I pray?

I pray in trust that
the act of prayer
is God's
designated way
of closing the
vast gulf
between infinity
and me.

13. Understanding The Lord's Prayer

THINK: Are you aware of what you are praying for when you say The Lord's Prayer?

The Lord's Prayer is recorded in both Matthew 6:9-13 and Luke 11:2-4. Matthew's account comes during the Sermon on the Mount and is told in connection with criticism of the flamboyant prayers of hypocrites and heathens. Luke's account is given in response to a request from one of Jesus' disciples, "Lord teach us to pray, as John taught his disciples." It is quite possible that these are two separate incidents.

Jesus was a man of prayer praying in private, in public, and on occasion spending whole nights in prayer. He often spoke to His disciples on the subject of prayer and cautioned them against doing it for show. Regarding prayer, Jesus urged perseverance, faith, and large expectations.

I like the way Philip Yancey in his book, Prayer: Does It Make A Difference "rewrote" the Lord's Prayer:

> *Dearest Lord:*
>
> *Remind me today that You live and reign, not in heaven only but all around me and in my life.*

May I "hallow" what lies before me, by consciously referring it to You, and also honor Your perfection, Your holiness, by seeking to become more like You.

May people believe in Your reign of goodness because of how I live today.

May I trust You for what I need today, nourishment for both body and soul, and not worry about future needs and wants.

Grant me to the same attitude of forgiving grace toward those who owe me, and who have wronged me, that You show toward me.

Let me not slide mindlessly toward evil today. Make me alert to its temptations and strong to resist it, with neither fear nor regret.

Please allow this to be so.

(Remember your prayer letter in the section "Prayer & The Right Kind of Requests"? It was modeled after the pattern of the Lord's Prayer as well.)

Interesting Facts:

- There are petitions or requests in this prayer. Some are directed toward God and His great purposes while others are directed toward our condition and wants.

- The opening expression, "Our Father" is particularly important as up until this point (throughout the Old Testament) God as Father was perceived as a to the nation as a whole. In Jesus' prayer, "Our Father" is personal and it is the first time where God is encouraged to be "our" individual Father in a close and personal sense.

- It was meant to be a lesson in prayer – a simple model to be followed. It surpassed all previous conceptions of how to pray to God and showed that a child of God could come in a simple direct manner to address our heavenly Father. For the new believer it provides a simple, instructive prayer. For the mature disciple it takes a lifetime to fully grasp the meaning and intent.

- The final lines of the prayer, known as the doxology ("For thine is the kingdom...") is not contained in Luke's version and is not in the earliest manuscripts of Matthew and most scholars do not consider it part of the original manuscript. The doxology has similarities to I Chronicles 29:11. Most Catholics do not include the doxology in the prayer while most Protestants do.

- The Lord's Prayer that Jesus prayed was meant to be a *pattern* as to how we pray not a chant. Each part of the prayer teaches us something about God, prayer, and our needs. Jesus didn't intend for us to recite it as if it were a magical incantation that would force God to do what we want Him to do and it should *never* be repeated mechanically, without thought; its purpose is to stimulate and awaken our faith.

Piece by Piece

The following are some other versions/translations of the Lord's Prayer including the original Aramaic language that Jesus spoke. Take the time to make note of each thing Jesus specifically prayed for. How many of them have come true as of today? You may be surprised.

1. **To Acknowledge** the might and power of God as well as our humble place. We should approach God as a respectful child approaches his father with humility and love. (Our Father …)

Version	Acknowledgement
King James Version	**OUR FATHER WHICH ART IN HEAVEN**
New Living Translation	Our Father in heaven
The Message	Our Father in heaven,
Original Aramaic	Our heavenly Father, hallowed is your name.

2. **To Honor** the supremacy of God. We are literally asking God to show us how holy, perfect and different from us He is. (Hallowed by …)

Version	1st Request: Universal Needs
King James Version	**HALLOWED BE THY NAME**
New Living Translation	may your name be honored.
The Message	Reveal who you are.
Original Aramaic	Your Kingdom is come.

3. **To Desire** God's plan and purpose to be achieved everywhere. God is the King. His desires (will) is what we are to obey. (Thy Kingdom come …)

Version	2nd Request: Earthly Needs
King James Version	**THY KINGDOM COME. THY WILL BE DONE IN EARTH, AS IT IS IN HEAVEN.**
New Living Translation	May your Kingdom come soon. May your will be done here on earth, just as it is in heaven.
The Message	Set the world right; Do what's best— as above, so below.
Original Aramaic	Your will is done, As in heaven so also on earth.

4. **To Trust** that God will provide everything you need. We do not ask for everything we want; we ask for everything we need. (Give us this day …)

Version	3rd Request: Personal Needs
King James Version	GIVE US THIS DAY OUR DAILY BREAD
New Living Translation	Give us our food for today,
The Message	Keep us alive with three square meals.
Original Aramaic	Give us the bread for our daily need.

5. **To Ask** for forgiveness from God in the same way you forgive others on earth. You cannot receive forgiveness if you don't admit that you need it! (And forgive us …)

Version	4th Request: Spiritual Needs
King James Version	AND FORGIVE US OUR DEBTS,
New Living Translation	and forgive us our sins,
The Message	Keep us forgiven with you.
Original Aramaic	And leave us serene,
Version	**5th Request: Worldly Needs**
King James Version	AS WE FORGIVE OUR DEBTORS.
New Living Translation	just as we have forgiven those who have sinned against us.
The Message	and forgiving others
Original Aramaic	just as we also allowed others serenity.

6. **To Ask** for strength and wisdom to recognize and resist all evil. We cannot do this on our own. We are fully dependent upon the Holy Spirit who lives in Christians to give us eyes that see the temptation and feet to escape it. (And lead us not…)

Version	6th Request: Individual Needs
King James Version	AND LEAD US NOT INTO TEMPTATION,
New Living Translation	And don't let us yield to temptation

The Message	Keep us safe from ourselves
Original Aramaic	And do not pass us through trial,

7. **To Surrender** yourself to God's Will, God's Direction, and God's Plan for your life. Technically, this wasn't in the Lord's Prayer in Luke's version (2:11-14) or in the earliest versions of Matthew (6:9-13). Taken from I Chronicles 29:11, it was added sometime later (When? Who knows...) and it closes out the prayer and declares God's holiness and sovereignty. (For thine is the Kingdom ...)

Version	7th Request: Admiration Needs
King James Version	FOR THINE IS THE KINGDOM, AND THE POWER, AND THE GLORY, FOR EVER
New Living Translation	For thine is the kingdom, and the power, and the glory, for ever.
The Message	You're in charge! You can do anything you want! You're ablaze in beauty!
Original Aramaic	For yours is the Kingdom, the Power and the Glory. To the end of the universe, of all the universes."

Have you ever thought of what the word, "Amen" means?

WHAT	Affirmation
King James Version	AMEN
New Living Translation	Amen.
The Message	Yes. Yes. Yes.
Original Aramaic	Yes, yes it will happen this way

THINK: Almost all of us know The Lord's Prayer from the King James Version of the Bible. Have you ever tried to write the Lord's Prayer in your own words? It's an interesting exercise that will really help you closely examine the different parts of a prayer that many of us have known by heart since childhood. Also, try www.biblegateway.com for many other free translations besides the few I've listed in this section.

Why do I pray?

Prayer allows me to see others as God sees them (and me): as uniquely flawed and uniquely gifted bearers of God's image.

14. Praying Other Biblical Prayers

Many people have trouble praying a loud. Others have trouble praying even quietly by themselves. If you struggle with formulating prayers, then try reading ones from the Bible. As you read them, pay attention to what ones speak the loudest to you. Which ones give you peace? Which ones make you feel powerful? In addition to the biblical prayers given in the previous chapters, here some more.

> Every human emotion and experience surges to the surface in the prayer-poems of Psalms.
>
> *(Yancey, 172)*

Daniel's Prayer of Confession

Daniel's entire city was attacked and all were taken prisoner, brought to an enemy land, and made to live in a society in which literally everything went again his people's spiritual beliefs. What did Daniel do? He prayed. (Daniel 9:3-19)

> *³ So I turned to the Lord God and pleaded with him in prayer and fasting. I also wore rough burlap and sprinkled myself with ashes.*

88

[4] *I prayed to the* LORD *my God and confessed:*

"O Lord, you are a great and awesome God! You always fulfill your covenant and keep your promises of unfailing love to those who love you and obey your commands. [5] *But we have sinned and done wrong. We have rebelled against you and scorned your commands and regulations.* [6] *We have refused to listen to your servants the prophets, who spoke on your authority to our kings and princes and ancestors and to all the people of the land.*

[7] *"Lord, you are in the right; but as you see, our faces are covered with shame. This is true of all of us, including the people of Judah and Jerusalem and all Israel, scattered near and far, wherever you have driven us because of our disloyalty to you.* [8] *O* LORD*, we and our kings, princes, and ancestors are covered with shame because we have sinned against you.* [9] *But the Lord our God is merciful and forgiving, even though we have rebelled against him.* [10] *We have not obeyed the* LORD *our God, for we have not followed the instructions he gave us through his servants the prophets.* [11] *All Israel has disobeyed your instruction and turned away, refusing to listen to your voice.*

"So now the solemn curses and judgments written in the Law of Moses, the servant of God, have been poured down on us because of our sin. [12] *You have kept your word and done to us and our rulers exactly as you warned. Never has there been such a*

disaster as happened in Jerusalem. [13] *Every curse written against us in the Law of Moses has come true. Yet we have refused to seek mercy from the* LORD *our God by turning from our sins and recognizing his truth.* [14] *Therefore, the* LORD *has brought upon us the disaster he prepared. The* LORD *our God was right to do all of these things, for we did not obey him.*

[15] *"O Lord our God, you brought lasting honor to your name by rescuing your people from Egypt in a great display of power. But we have sinned and are full of wickedness.* [16] *In view of all your faithful mercies, Lord, please turn your furious anger away from your city Jerusalem, your holy mountain. All the neighboring nations mock Jerusalem and your people because of our sins and the sins of our ancestors.*

[17] *"O our God, hear your servant's prayer! Listen as I plead. For your own sake, Lord, smile again on your desolate sanctuary.*

[18] *"O my God, lean down and listen to me. Open your eyes and see our despair. See how your city— the city that bears your name—lies in ruins. We make this plea, not because we deserve help, but because of your mercy.*

[19] *"O Lord, hear. O Lord, forgive. O Lord, listen and act! For your own sake, do not delay, O my God, for your people and your city bear your name."*

Why do I pray?

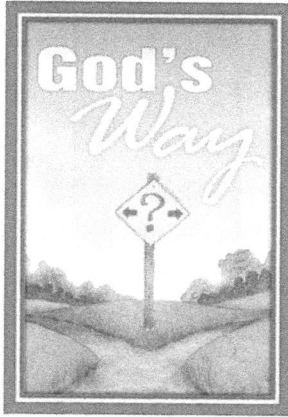

I pray always and only for the Lord's Will. I make suggestions and share my desires, but always acknowledge that He Knows Best. Certainly He has to have the best plan for the future and the best solution to any problem. **Wouldn't it be the greatest possible disaster to argue with God and win?**

Hannah's Prayer for a Son

Hannah wanted a son more than anything else. In deep anguish and crying bitterly she prayed to the Lord and made the following promise. (I Samuel 1:11) God would give her a son and she would keep her promise. Her son, Samuel, would become one of God's greatest prophets.

> [11] *And she made this vow: "O LORD of Heaven's Armies, if you will look upon my sorrow and answer my prayer and give me a son, then I will give him back to you. He will be yours for his entire lifetime, and as a sign that he has been dedicated to the LORD, his hair will never be cut."*

Why do I pray?

God needs no reminding of the nature of reality, but I certainly do.

David's Prayer of Praise

He slayed Goliath when he was a boy, was a shepherd, a fierce warrior, and eventually was crowned the second king of Israel. He also wrote beautiful psalms – sacred songs or hymns. Here are three of them.

Psalm 45:8-13

> The LORD is merciful and compassionate, slow to get angry and filled with unfailing love.
> [9] The LORD is good to everyone. He showers compassion on all his creation.
> [10] All of your works will thank you, LORD, and your faithful followers will praise you.
> [11] They will speak of the glory of your kingdom; they will give examples of your power.
> [12] They will tell about your mighty deeds and about the majesty and glory of your reign.

[13] *For your kingdom is an everlasting kingdom. You rule throughout all generations.*

David's Prayer of Acknowledgement

Psalm 63

63 God! My God! It's you—I search for you! My whole being thirsts for you! My body desires you in a dry and tired land, no water anywhere.
[2] *Yes, I've seen you in the sanctuary; I've seen your power and glory.*
[3] *My lips praise you because your faithful love is better than life itself!*
[4] *So I will bless you as long as I'm alive; I will lift up my hands in your name.*

[5] *I'm fully satisfied—as with a rich dinner. My mouth speaks praise with joy on my lips—*
[6] *whenever I ponder you on my bed, whenever I meditate on you in the middle of the night—*
[7] *because you've been a help to me and I shout for joy in the protection of your wings.*
[8] *My whole being clings to you; your strong hand upholds me.*

David's Prayer of Surrender

Psalm 139

[1] *O Lᴏʀᴅ, you have examined my heart and know everything about me.*
[2] *You know when I sit down or stand up. You know*

my thoughts even when I'm far away.

3 You see me when I travel and when I rest at home. You know everything I do.

4 You know what I am going to say even before I say it, LORD.

5 You go before me and follow me. You place your hand of blessing on my head.

6 Such knowledge is too wonderful for me, too great for me to understand!

7 I can never escape from your Spirit! I can never get away from your presence!

8 If I go up to heaven, you are there; if I go down to the grave, you are there.

9 If I ride the wings of the morning, if I dwell by the farthest oceans,

10 even there your hand will guide me, and your strength will support me.

11 I could ask the darkness to hide me and the light around me to become night—

12 but even in darkness I cannot hide from you. To you the night shines as bright as day. Darkness and light are the same to you.

13 You made all the delicate, inner parts of my body and knit me together in my mother's womb.

14 Thank you for making me so wonderfully complex! Your workmanship is marvelous—how well I know it.

15 You watched me as I was being formed in utter seclusion, as I was woven together in the dark of the womb.

¹⁶ You saw me before I was born. Every day of my life was recorded in your book. Every moment was laid out before a single day had passed.

¹⁷ How precious are your thoughts about me, O God. They cannot be numbered!
¹⁸ I can't even count them; they outnumber the grains of sand! And when I wake up, you are still with me!

¹⁹ O God, if only you would destroy the wicked! Get out of my life, you murderers!
²⁰ They blaspheme you; your enemies misuse your name.
²¹ O LORD, shouldn't I hate those who hate you? Shouldn't I despise those who oppose you?
²² Yes, I hate them with total hatred, for your enemies are my enemies.

²³ Search me, O God, and know my heart; test me and know my anxious thoughts.
²⁴ Point out anything in me that offends you, and lead me along the path of everlasting life.

Why do I pray?

Because prayer doesn't fit me for a greater work; **prayer is the greater work.**

Nehemiah's Prayer for Success

Nehemiah was responsible for overseeing the rebuilding of Jerusalem and purifying the Jewish community after the King of Persia allowed the Jews to return and rebuild the city of Jerusalem about 440 B.C.. He became governor of the province and managed to rebuild the walls within 52 days. (Nehemiah 1:5-11)

"O LORD, God of heaven, the great and awesome God who keeps his covenant of unfailing love with those who love him and obey his commands, [6] listen to my prayer! Look down and see me praying night and day for your people Israel. I confess that we have sinned against you. Yes, even my own family and I have sinned! [7] We have sinned terribly by not obeying the commands, decrees, and regulations that you gave us through your servant Moses.

[8] "Please remember what you told your servant Moses: 'If you are unfaithful to me, I will scatter

you among the nations. ⁹ But if you return to me and obey my commands and live by them, then even if you are exiled to the ends of the earth, I will bring you back to the place I have chosen for my name to be honored.'

¹⁰ "The people you rescued by your great power and strong hand are your servants. ¹¹ O Lord, please hear my prayer! Listen to the prayers of those of us who delight in honoring you. Please grant me success today by making the king favorable to me. Put it into his heart to be kind to me."

Why do I pray?

I pray in astonished belief that God desires an ongoing relationship with me.

Ezra's Prayer of Intercession For Israel

In 458 B.C. Ezra returned from being exiled in Babylonia to Jerusalem where he reintroduced the Torah and cleansed the community of mixed marriages. (Ezra 9:5-15)

⁵ At the time of the sacrifice, I stood up from where I had sat in mourning with my clothes torn. I fell to

my knees and lifted my hands to the LORD my God.
[6] I prayed,

"O my God, I am utterly ashamed; I blush to lift up
my face to you. For our sins are piled higher than
our heads, and our guilt has reached to the
heavens. [7] From the days of our ancestors until
now, we have been steeped in sin. That is why we
and our kings and our priests have been at the
mercy of the pagan kings of the land. We have
been killed, captured, robbed, and disgraced, just
as we are today.

[8] "But now we have been given a brief moment of
grace, for the LORD our God has allowed a few of us
to survive as a remnant. He has given us security in
this holy place. Our God has brightened our eyes
and granted us some relief from our slavery. [9] For
we were slaves, but in his unfailing love our God did
not abandon us in our slavery. Instead, he caused
the kings of Persia to treat us favorably. He revived
us so we could rebuild the Temple of our God and
repair its ruins. He has given us a protective wall in
Judah and Jerusalem.

[10] "And now, O our God, what can we say after all
of this? For once again we have abandoned your
commands! [11] Your servants the prophets warned
us when they said, 'The land you are entering to
possess is totally defiled by the detestable practices
of the people living there. From one end to the
other, the land is filled with corruption. [12] Don't let

your daughters marry their sons! Don't take their daughters as wives for your sons. Don't ever promote the peace and prosperity of those nations. If you follow these instructions, you will be strong and will enjoy the good things the land produces, and you will leave this prosperity to your children forever.'

[13] "Now we are being punished because of our wickedness and our great guilt. But we have actually been punished far less than we deserve, for you, our God, have allowed some of us to survive as a remnant. [14] But even so, we are again breaking your commands and intermarrying with people who do these detestable things. Won't your anger be enough to destroy us, so that even this little remnant no longer survives? [15] O LORD, God of Israel, you are just. We come before you in our guilt as nothing but an escaped remnant, though in such a condition none of us can stand in your presence."

THINK: How are these ancient biblical prayers different from your prayers? How are they the same?

Why do I pray?

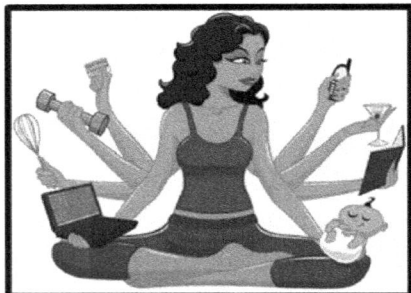

With the Right Attitude and the Right Guidance I can pray almost constantly. I can pray when I talk to people by letting the Lord lead my conversations. I can pray when I read my Bible by offering up my heart and thoughts to Him for enlightenment. I can pray in the car, in the line at the store, as I wash dishes and change sheets, while I eat lunch or pull weeds in my garden by willingly giving my actions over to God and letting Him lead so I can follow.

15. Types of Prayers

Supplication Prayers

Determine to pray about something instead of worrying about something.

Trust God's promise that He can replace your anxiety with a spirit of peace big enough to guard both your heart and your mind.

Determine to transfer your fear, anxiety, and impatience to God.

- Personality struggles, trials, finances, family relationships, goals and dreams, cars, friendships, homes, vacations, lost contacts, emotional hurts...the list goes on and on... Whenever you feel that overwhelmed, dull feeling in your stomach or feel bombarded with too many stress producing thoughts, you should simply pray. Admit your anxieties, relinquish your worries, and request His provisions for escape ... in big or small situations.

Scripture about Supplication Prayers:

- Luke 11:1-4 Jesus said, "This is how you should pray: "Father, may your name be kept holy. May your Kingdom come soon. [3] Give us each day the food we need, [4] and forgive us our sins, as we forgive those who sin against us. And don't let us yield to temptation."

- James 4:2 2You want what you don't have, so you scheme and kill to get it. You are jealous for what others have, and you can't possess it, so you fight and quarrel to take it away from them. And yet the reason you don't have what you want is that you don't ask God for it. NLT

- Philippians 4:6 6Don't worry about anything; instead, pray about everything. Tell God what you need, and thank him for all he has done. NLT

- Psalm 23:4 Even when I walk through the darkest valley, I will not be afraid, for you are close beside me. Your rod and your staff protect and comfort me.

- I Peter 5:7-8 Give all your worries and cares to God, for he cares about you. 8 Stay alert! Watch out for your great enemy, the devil. He prowls around like a roaring lion, looking for someone to devour.

- Psalm 130:6 I long for the Lord more than sentries long for the dawn, yes, more than sentries long for the dawn.

- Psalm 119:82-84 My eyes are straining to see your promises come true. When will you comfort me? [83] I am shriveled like a wineskin in the smoke, but I have not forgotten to obey your decrees. [84] How long must I wait? When will you punish those who persecute me?

Believing Prayers

Look for God to do the impossible. The extraordinary. The Unbelievable. Why not? He's <u>GOD.</u>

<u>Oh, to believe God for the impossible in our lives</u> – not because we deserve it but because of His awesome love – and to allow Him to be glorified in the results is an extremely challenging but powerful prayer principle for those who believe! We are to put our believe in the Promiser – in God's power, love, and faithfulness.

Scripture about Believing Prayers:

- Matthew 21:22 22If you believe, you will receive whatever you ask for in prayer. NLT

- Habakkuk 1:5 5The LORD replied, "Look at the nations and be amazed! Watch and be astounded at what I will do! For I am doing something in your own day, something you wouldn't believe even if someone told you about it. NLT

Why do I pray?

So God can show me what He's doing today, and how I can be part of it.

Revealing Prayers

Ask God to help you pray when you are unsure of which direction He wishes you to go.

<u>Rather than trying to convince God of something, ask Him to convince you of His will.</u> Once feeling His assurance, through (1)

Scripture, (2) His Spirit and yours agreeing, and (3) the godly counsel of other Christians, you're encouraged to wait until He brings the blessing of His answer. Having no time limits, this principle can become a month- to a year-long process in the case of certain requests.

Scripture about Revealing Prayers:

- James 1:2-6 2Dear brothers and sisters, whenever trouble comes your way, let it be an opportunity for joy. 3For when your faith is tested, your endurance has a chance to grow. 4So let it grow, for when your endurance is fully developed, you will be strong in character and ready for anything. 5If you need wisdom--if you want to know what God wants you to do--ask him, and he will gladly tell you. He will not resent your asking. 6But when you ask him, be sure that you really expect him to answer, for a doubtful mind is as unsettled as a wave of the sea that is driven and tossed by the wind. NLT

Interceding Prayers

Never stop praying. But trust that God is in charge of the results.

Specific prayers for the needs and desires of family, friends, coworkers, Christian organizations, and those we may not even know.

Scripture about Interceding Prayers:

- Colossians 1:9-12 9So we have continued praying for you ever since we first heard about you. We ask God to give you a complete understanding of what he wants to do in your lives, and we ask him to make you wise with spiritual wisdom. 10Then the way you live will always honor and please the Lord, and you will continually do good, kind things for others. All the while, you will learn to know God better and better. 11We also pray that you will be strengthened with his glorious power so that you will have all the patience and endurance you need. May you be filled with joy, 12always thanking the Father, who has enabled you to share the inheritance that belongs to God's holy people, who live in the light.

Why do I pray?

Because the habit of <u>not</u> praying is far more difficult to break than the habit of praying.

Corporate Prayers

Become a prayer partner with someone.

<u>Praying *with others* for God's intervention in any given situation creates excitement and incentive to keep agreeing in prayer! Pg. 117</u>

Agreeing prayer can become contagious when others around you see God's hand moving in incredible, sometimes seemingly impossible, situations. From large to small agreeing prayers, God continually shows us that He is listening and faithful and that the size of the request is insignificant.

Scripture about Corporate Prayers:

- Matthew 18:19 19"I also tell you this: If two of you agree down here on earth concerning anything you ask, my Father in heaven will do it for you. NLT

Why do I pray?

I pray in order to put myself in the stream of God's healing work on earth.

Persevering Prayers

Don't let life steal from your prayer time.

<u>The secret of perseverance is patience and faith, waiting and hasting.</u>

It is fair to acknowledge that one's faith is greatly challenged to grow during trials. Prayer then becomes the avenue of daily released the anxieties of humanly irreversible situations to God and sensing His presence amidst the unknown.

Scripture about Persevering Prayers:

- Luke 18:1-8 1 One day Jesus told his disciples a story to illustrate their need for constant prayer and to show them that they must never give up. 2"There was a judge in a certain city," he said, "who was a godless man with great contempt for everyone. 3A widow of that city came to him repeatedly, appealing for justice against someone who had harmed her. 4The judge ignored her for a while, but eventually she wore him out. `I fear neither God nor man,' he said to himself, 5`but this woman is driving me crazy. I'm going to see that she gets justice, because she is wearing me out with her constant requests!' " 6Then the Lord said, "Learn a lesson from this evil judge. 7Even he rendered a just decision in the end, so don't you think God will surely give justice to his chosen people who plead with him day and night? Will he keep putting them off? 8I tell you, he will grant justice to them quickly! But when I, the Son of Man, return, how many will I find who have faith?" NLT

- Hebrews 11:1 1What is faith? It is the confident assurance that what we hope for is going to happen. It is the evidence of things we cannot yet see. NLT

Why do I pray?

I pray to give an opportunity for God to say, "yes", "no", or "not right now." God is not really silent, we are deaf. **Some of God's greatest gifts are unanswered prayers, you know.**

Prayers of Thanksgiving/Worship

Always, always begin your prayer with thanks and appreciate for all God has blessed you with.

Prayers of thanksgiving and worship are very similar. The difference is that prayers of worship focus on who God is while thanksgiving focuses on what God has done.

Scripture about Thanksgiving/Worship Prayers:

- Philippians 4:6 [6] Don't worry about anything; instead, pray about everything. Tell God what you need, and thank him for all he has done.

- I Thessalonians 1:2 We always thank God for all of you and pray for you constantly.

- Colossians 1:3 We always pray for you, and we give thanks to God, the Father of our Lord Jesus Christ.

- Psalm 95:6-7 Come, let us worship and bow down. Let us kneel before the LORD our maker,
  [7] for he is our God. We are the people he watches over, the flock under his care. If only you would listen to his voice today!

Why do I pray?

I believe I can accomplish more for the world by praying faithfully than by walking into the White House, or Whitehall, or the Kremlin with suggestions.

Prayers of Consecration

Commit your works to the Lord. (And your plans will be established. Proverbs 16:3)

Prayers of consecration involves a time in which we set ourselves apart from others to follow God's will. Jesus made such a prayer the night before His Crucifixion.

Scripture about Consecration Prayers:

- Matthew 26:39 He went on a little farther and bowed with his face to the ground, praying, "My Father! If it is possible, let this cup of suffering be taken away from me. Yet I want your will to be done, not mine."

- Isaiah 6:8 Then I heard the Lord asking, "Whom should I send as a messenger to this people? Who will go for us?" I said, "Here I am. Send me."

THINK: How many types of prayers do you actually pray?

Why do I pray?

Because God is alive all day, living both around me and inside me, speaking in a still, small voice and in other ways I may not even recognize.

109

16. Prayer Ideas

Develop a method to list those things that come to you over the course of the day that concern you or catch your attention and that you recognize as something you can pray for.

Try praying for (in no particular order!)

- For our Leaders.
- Our soldiers (and their families).
- Those with have no one else to pray for them.
- The homeless and the poor and the sick and the elderly.
- For your church leaders.
- For your neighbors.
- For the people you interact with every day – the ones you like and the ones you don't!
- For God's Missionaries around the world.
- For those who have never had the opportunity to hear The Truth about God.
- For opportunities for you to tell others your story.
- For opportunities for you to serve.
- That you will see the world through God's perspective.
- That all you do will honor and please God in all you do.
- That God will keep those He wishes you to have in your life close and remove those He wishes you to not have in your life.

- That God will show you Big Black Arrows (clear direction and no confusion) as to what He wants you to do and where He wants you to go.

- For those who have been unkind to you.

- For those you struggle to forgive.

- For those you have hurt or wronged.

- For God to clearly communicate to you what else He wishes you to bring to Him in prayer.

Why do I pray?

I pray because I believe prayer is a subversive act in a world that constantly calls faith into question ... and **I like to go against the world whenever I get the opportunity.**

17. Your Personal Prayer Plan

When I will try to pray daily: (Give a length of time estimate, too.)	
Where I will try to pray daily:	
How I will remember what to pray for daily:	
What I will pray for daily:	**Pray:** • Acknowledge the might and power of God. • Honoring God, recognizing how perfect and different God is from us. • Trusting that God will provide everything you need. • Asking for forgiveness just as you have forgiven others. • Asking for strength and wisdom to do what is right and avoid what is wrong. • Asking for God's will regarding your life's direction and regarding any requests or needs that you have.

In addition, I will pray for:

What change I would hope to see in myself as a result of this improved prayer life	
In addition to prayer, I will make a point to (devotions, memorize scripture?)	
I will have a prayer partner	
My prayer partner will be	

18.   Some Scripture about Prayer

Exodus 23:13 "Be sure to obey all my instructions. And remember, never pray to or swear by any other gods. Do not even mention their names.

Psalm 5:2 Listen to my cry for help, my King and my God, for I will never pray to anyone but you.

Psalm 119:145 I pray with all my heart; answer me, LORD! I will obey your principles.

Psalm 138:3 When I pray, you answer me; you encourage me by giving me the strength I need.

Jeremiah 29:12 In those days when you pray, I will listen.

Matthew 5:44 But I say, love your enemies! Pray for those who persecute you!

> The entire Bible chronicles God's effort to renew what was lost on that day in the garden when Adam hid and no longer conversed with God as a friend. One day we will all have that chance.
>
> *(Yancey, 328)*

Luke 6:28 Pray for the happiness of those who curse you. Pray for those who hurt you.

Romans 12:14 If people persecute you because you are a Christian, don't curse them; pray that God will bless them.

Matthew 6:5 [*Teaching about Prayer and Fasting*] "And now about prayer. When you pray, don't be like the hypocrites who love to pray publicly on street corners and in the synagogues where everyone can see them. I assure you, that is all the reward they will ever get.

Matthew 6:6 But when you pray, go away by yourself, shut the door behind you, and pray to your Father secretly. Then your Father, who knows all secrets, will reward you.

Matthew 6:7 "When you pray, don't babble on and on as people of other religions do. They think their prayers are answered only by repeating their words again and again.

Matthew 6:9 Pray like this: Our Father in heaven, may your name be honored.

Luke 11:2 He said, "This is how you should pray: "Father, may your name be honored. May your Kingdom come soon.

Matthew 26:41 Keep alert and pray. Otherwise temptation will overpower you. For though the spirit is willing enough, the body is weak!"

Mark 14:38 Keep alert and pray. Otherwise temptation will overpower you. For though the spirit is willing enough, the body is weak."

Mark 11:24 Listen to me! You can pray for anything, and if you believe, you will have it.

Luke 10:2 These were his instructions to them: "The harvest is so great, but the workers are so few. Pray to the Lord who is in charge of the harvest, and ask him to send out more workers for his fields.

Romans 1:9 God knows how often I pray for you. Day and night I bring you and your needs in prayer to God, whom I serve with all my heart by telling others the Good News about his Son.

Romans 1:10 One of the things I always pray for is the opportunity, God willing, to come at last to see you.

2 Corinthians 13:9 We are glad to be weak, if you are really strong. What we pray for is your restoration to maturity.

2 Corinthians 10:4 We use God's mighty weapons, not worldly weapons, to knock down the strongholds of human reasoning and to destroy false arguments.

Ephesians 1:16 I have never stopped thanking God for you. I pray for you constantly,

Ephesians 1:18 I pray that your hearts will be flooded with light so that you can understand the wonderful future he has promised to those he called. I want you to realize what a rich and glorious inheritance he has given to his people.

Ephesians 1:19 I pray that you will begin to understand the incredible greatness of his power for us who believe him. This is the same mighty power

Ephesians 3:16 I pray that from his glorious, unlimited resources he will give you mighty inner strength through his Holy Spirit.

Ephesians 3:17 And I pray that Christ will be more and more at home in your hearts as you trust in him. May your roots go down deep into the soil of God's marvelous love.

Ephesians 6:18 Pray at all times and on every occasion in the power of the Holy Spirit. Stay alert and be persistent in your prayers for all Christians everywhere.

Ephesians 6:19 And pray for me, too. Ask God to give me the right words as I boldly explain God's secret plan that the Good News is for the Gentiles, too.

Philippians 1:9 I pray that your love for each other will overflow more and more, and that you will keep on growing in your knowledge and understanding.

Philippians 4:6 Don't worry about anything; instead, pray about everything. Tell God what you need, and thank him for all he has done.

Colossians 1:11 We also pray that you will be strengthened with his glorious power so that you will have all the patience and endurance you need. May you be filled with joy,

Colossians 4:3 Don't forget to pray for us, too, that God will give us many opportunities to preach about his secret plan--that Christ is also for you Gentiles. That is why I am here in chains.

Colossians 4:4 Pray that I will proclaim this message as clearly as I should.

1 Thessalonians 1:2 [*The Faith of the Thessalonian Believers*] We always thank God for all of you and pray for you constantly.

2 Thessalonians 1:11 And so we keep on praying for you, that our God will make you worthy of the life to which he called you. And we pray that God, by his power, will fulfill all your good intentions and faithful deeds.

2 Thessalonians 3:1 [*Pauls Request for Prayer*] Finally, dear brothers and sisters, I ask you to pray for us. Pray first that the Lord's message will spread rapidly and be honored wherever it goes, just as when it came to you.

2 Thessalonians 3:2 Pray, too, that we will be saved from wicked and evil people, for not everyone believes in the Lord.

1 Timothy 2:1 [*Instructions about Worship*] I urge you, first of all, to pray for all people. As you make your requests, plead for God's mercy upon them, and give thanks.

1 Timothy 2:2 Pray this way for kings and all others who are in authority, so that we can live in peace and quietness, in godliness and dignity.

Hebrews 13:18 Pray for us, for our conscience is clear and we want to live honorably in everything we do.

James 5:16 Confess your sins to each other and pray for each other so that you may be healed. The earnest prayer of a righteous person has great power and wonderful results.

1 Peter 1:17 And remember that the heavenly Father to whom you pray has no favorites when he judges. He will judge or reward you according to what you do. So you must live in reverent fear of him during your time as foreigners here on earth.

Jude 1:20 But you, dear friends, must continue to build your lives on the foundation of your holy faith. And continue to pray as you are directed by the Holy Spirit.

Matthew 7:7 [*Effective Prayer*] "Keep on asking, and you will be given what you ask for. Keep on looking, and you will find. Keep on knocking, and the door will be opened.

Matthew 21:22 If you believe, you will receive whatever you ask for in prayer."

James 5:13 [*The Power of Prayer*] Are any among you suffering? They should keep on praying about it. And those who have reason to be thankful should continually sing praises to the Lord.

James 5:15 And their prayer offered in faith will heal the sick, and the Lord will make them well. And anyone who has committed sins will be forgiven.

James 5:16 Confess your sins to each other and pray for each other so that you may be healed. The earnest prayer of a righteous person has great power and wonderful results.

Jude 1:24 [*A Prayer of Praise*] And now, all glory to God, who is able to keep you from stumbling, and who will bring you into his glorious presence innocent of sin and with great joy.

Why do I pray?

If prayer stands
as a place
where God
and human
beings meet,
then I must
pray.

19. Prayer Quotes

Who one believes God to be is most accurately revealed not in any credo but in the way one speaks to God when no one else is listening. ~Nancy Mairs

Why should I ask of him that he would change for me the course of things? I who ought to love, above all, the order established by his wisdom and maintained by his Providence, shall I wish that order to be dissolved on my account? Rousseau

I have a notion that what seems our worst prayers may really be, in God's eyes, our best. Those, I mean, which are least supported by devotional feeling and contend with the greatest disinclination. For these, perhaps, being nearly all will, come from a deeper level than feeling. ~C.S. Lewis

Keeping company with God includes far more than the time I devote to prayer each day. God is alive all day, living both around me and inside me, speaking in a still, small voice and in other ways I may not even recognize. ~Philip Yancey

God is not really silent, we are deaf. ~Teresa of Avila.

"Create space in which God can act." Henry Nouwen

"The longer I live, the more convincing proofs I see of this truth, that God governs in the affairs of men." ~George Washington

You shall love God with everything you have and everything you are. Everything. Every longing, every endowment, each of your intellectual gifts, any athletic talent or computer skill, all capacity for delight, every good thing that has your fingerprints on it – take all this, says Jesus, and refer it to God. Take your longing, and long for God: take your creaturely riches, and endow God; take your eye for beauty and appreciate God. With your heart and soul and mind, with all your needs and splendors, make a full turn toward God. ~Plantings

O gracious and holy Father, give us wisdom to perceive Thee, intelligence to understand Thee, diligence to see Thee, patience to wait for Thee, eyes to behold Thee, a heart to meditate upon Thee, and a life to proclaim Thee; through the power of the Spirit of Jesus Christ our Lord. ~Benedict of Nursia

Pray as if everything depended upon God and work as if everything depended upon man. Francis Cardinal Spellman (1889 - 1967)

You can pray for someone even if you don't think God exists. Real Live Preacher, *RealLivePreacher.com Weblog, July 7, 2003*

There are more tears shed over answered prayers than over unanswered prayers. ~Saint Theresa of Jesus

No one is a firmer believer in the power of prayer than the devil; not that he practices it, but he suffers from it. ~Guy H. King

Don't pray when it rains if you don't pray when the sun shines. ~Satchel Paige, 1974

Deep down in me I knowed it was a lie, and He knowed it. You can't pray a lie - I found that out. ~Mark Twain

Most people do not pray; they only beg. ~George Bernard Shaw

Prayer & Me

There is a mighty lot of difference between saying prayers and praying. ~John G. Lake

When I pray, coincidences happen, and when I don't pray, they don't. ~William Temple

There is nothing that makes us love a man so much as praying for him. ~William Law

Prayer does not fit us for the greater work, prayer *is* the greater work. ~Oswald Chambers

Groanings which cannot be uttered are often prayers which cannot be refused. ~ *Spurgeon*

Men may spurn our appeals, reject our message, oppose our arguments, despise our persons; but they are helpless against our prayers. ~J. Sidlow Baxter

Why do I pray?

I pray with an open heart and an open mind. After all, **God cannot fill what has not been emptied.** God is more creative, more powerful, and more clever than I could ever imagine so I'd rather go with His Ideas. Plus, He's got a great sense of humor.

20. Personal Prayer Survey

Just to make you think...

Part I: Me & God

1. **The ultimate authority in my life is**

   My family's survival

   My needs minute by minute

   God's eternity

2. **I operate by**

   God's timeline

   My timeline

3. **The laws of genetics**

   Should be disbanded based on my person whim

   Should be disbanded only according to God's timeline

4. **I would describe my relationship with God as**

   Distant

   Acquaintance

   Friendship

   Partnership

5. **If you carried on the same kind of relationship with your friends that you have with God, do you think you would have more or fewer friends than you do now?**

   More

   Fewer

   Same

Part II: YOUR PRAYERS IN GENERAL:

6. **My purpose for praying is so**

   I can pose a request to God

   I can establish a relationship with God

7. **I want God to fulfill prayers**

   Even if He knows they are not in my best interest

   That I think are best

   That He thinks are best

8. **I understand what I should and shouldn't pray for.**

   No

   I think I do

   Yes

9. **My prayers make a difference.**

   No

   I think they do.

   Yes

10. The frequency of unanswered prayers in my life is

All the time. My prayers never get answered.

Sometimes. I just never know.

Never. Every single one of my prayers are faithfully answered. What was your most recent victory through prayer?

11. Is your prayer life better now than it was a year ago?

Yes

No

12. Jesus lived a perfect life on earth, connecting with His Father through prayer, and relying on Him for wisdom and power. Do you think it is possible for us to have the same kind of relationship with God?

Yes

No

13. What do you think prayer does for you personally?

Nothing so far

It gets me things I need and want

It keeps me on the right track spiritually

It makes me feel closer to God

It helps me better understand myself

It helps me understand God's will better

14. Do you sense the presence of God when you pray?

Never

Sometimes

Always

15. Do you find your prayers satisfying?

> Never
>
> Sometimes
>
> Always

Part III: YOUR STYLE:

16. Do you have a quiet time with God where you only listen?

> Yes
>
> No
>
> Sometimes

17. How often should you pray

> 3 times a day like Daniel
>
> at least once a day
>
> whenever you need to
>
> on very special occasions
>
> when you've come to the end of your own resources
>
> only when you come to church
>
> many times a day

18. Think about the prayers you usually pray. What is the focus of your prayers?

> myself and my needs

> my family and its needs

> my friends and their needs

> the world and its needs

> thanksgiving and praise for God's goodness

19. What time of day do you pray?

> I don't pray

> Early AM

> Mid-Morning

> Afternoon

> Evening

> After Midnight

> No Special Time, it always varies

20. How long do you spend in prayer each day?(Circle your answer)

> Too little to time

> 15 Minutes

> 30 Minutes

> 1 Hour

> More than 1 Hour

21. What is your posture in prayer?

Kneeling

Walking

Lying down

Sitting quietly

Anyway I can

22. Do you have a specific place where you pray each day?

Yes

No

If Yes, where?

23. Do you regularly pray for (circle all that apply)

the persecuted church?

for the pastors and teachers of your church?

for the missionaries of your church?

for souls to be saved?

for your children?

for your spouse?

for worldwide revival?

24. Do you have a prayer partner?

Yes

No

Part IV: YOUR EXTENDED PRAYER ACTIVITIES:

25. Do you read your Bible during your prayer time?

Yes

No

26. Do you read through the Bible each year?

Yes

No

Never have

27. Do you use a devotional in your prayer time?

Yes

No

If yes, what is the name of your current devotional?

28. Do you routinely keep a prayer journal?

Yes

No

29. Do you fast?

Yes

No

Sometimes

30. Do you memorize Scriptures?

Yes

No

Sometimes

31. **What do you think Jesus would have you change or adjust with your prayer time while participating in this Bible Study?**

Part V: PRAYER TRIVIA:

32. **"Amen" means**

   The End

   Surely, indeed, truly

   Please, allow this to be so

   All of the above

33. **A prayer is**

   A fervent request

   Said only in silence

   Can only be directed to a deity

   None of the above

34. **Which is an example of prayer to God?**

   Confession of sins

   Songs of praise

   Words of devotion or gratitude

   All of the above

Susan McGeown

35. The Lord's Prayer

Was Jesus' "how to" instruction guide

Must be said daily

Is an adaptation of an ancient Jewish prayer

All of the above

http://www.wgbd.org/prayer-assessment.html

http://cornerstoneconnections.adventist.org/CornerTchr/2006/Q2/Q2_06_CCTGLesson6.pdf#searc h=%22prayer%20questionnaire%22

Why do I pray?

I make the effort
to maintain a ground of oceanic silence
out of which arises the multitude of phenomena of
daily life.
I make the effort
to see and to passionately open in love to the
spirit that infuses all things.
I make the effort
to see the Beloved in everyone
and to serve the Beloved through everyone
(including the earth).
I often fail in these aspirations
because I lose the balance between
separateness and unity,
get lost in my separateness,
and feel afraid.
But I make the effort. Ram Dass

21. Prayer Resources

Prayer: Does It Make Any Difference?, By Philip Yancey, Zondervan Publishers, 2010 ISBN 978-0310328889 READ THIS BOOK IT IS TERRIFIC.

New Living Translation Bible, Tyndale House Foundation, Carol Stream, Illinois, 2013

www.biblegateway.com

http://www.wgbd.org/prayer-assessment.htmlhttp://cornerstoneconnections.adventist.org/CornerTchr/2006/Q2/Q2_06_CCTGLesson6.pdf#search=%22prayer%20questionnaire%22

http://www.str.org/site/News2?page=NewsArticle&id=5648

http://www.gnmagazine.org/issues/gn59/prayerlife.htm

About The Author

Susan McGeown is a wife, mother, daughter, sister, friend, aunt, uncle (don't ask), teacher, author … but, most importantly, a "woman after God's own heart." Always working on a new book, she has five historical novels (including *Rosamund's Bower,* 2008 RCRW's Golden Rose winner in the category of 'Novel with Romantic Elements'), seven contemporary fiction novels, and seven nonfiction Bible studies (at last count anyway). She's been a teacher, a conference leader, a public speaker, a Children's minister, a deacon, an elder, a vacation Bible school coordinator, a preschool director, and a Bible study leader yet writing stories is just about the best way she can imagine spending her time. Living in Bridgewater, New Jersey, with her husband of over twenty years and their three children, each of Sue's stories champions those emotions nearest and dearest to her: faith, joy, hope and love.

Philippians 1:20-21

Why do I pray?

Make of your life an offering!
Make of your life a prayer!
Be awake to the Life that is loving you and sing your prayer, laugh your prayer,
Dance your prayer, run and weep and sweat your prayer,
Sleep your prayer, eat your prayer,
Pain, sculpt, hammer, and read your prayer,
Sweep, dig, rake, drive, and hoe your prayer,
Garden and farm and build and clean your prayer
Wash, iron, vacuum, sew, embroider, and pickle your prayer,
Compute, touch, bend, and fold but never delete or mutilate your prayer.

Learn and pray your prayer,
Work and rest your prayer,
Fast and feast your prayer,
Argue, talk, whisper, listen, and shout your prayer,
Groan and moan and spit and sneeze your prayer,
Swim and hunt and cook your prayer,
Digest and become your prayer,
Release and recover your prayer,
Breathe your prayer,
Be your prayer.

Ada Renee Bozarth

www.ingramcontent.com/pod-product-compliance
Lightning Source LLC
Chambersburg PA
CBHW061730020426
42331CB00006B/1177